Understanding Jesus Today

JESUS AND THE FUTURE

Understanding Jesus Today

Edited by Howard Clark Kee

Growing interest in the historical Jesus can be frustrated by diverse and conflicting claims about what he said and did. This series brings together in accessible form the conclusions of an international team of distinguished scholars regarding various important aspects of Jesus' teaching. All of the authors have extensively analyzed the biblical and contextual evidence about who Jesus was and what he taught, and they summarize their findings here in easily readable and stimulating discussions. Each book includes an appendix of questions for further thought and recommendations for further reading on the topic covered.

Other Books in the Series

Jesus and the Future

DAVID TIEDE

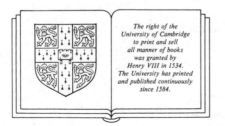

The right of the
University of Cambridge
to print and sell
all manner of books
was granted by
Henry VIII in 1534.
The University has printed
and published continuously
since 1584.

CAMBRIDGE UNIVERSITY PRESS

Cambridge
New York   Port Chester   Melbourne   Sydney

Published by the Press Syndicate of the University of Cambridge
The Pitt Building, Trumpington Street, Cambridge CB2 1RP
40 West 20th Street, New York, NY 10011, USA
10 Stamford Road, Oakleigh, Melbourne 3166, Australia

First published 1990

Printed in the United States of America

Library of Congress Cataloging-in-Publication Data
Tiede, David Lenz.
Jesus and the future / David Tiede.
   p.   cm. – (Understanding Jesus today)
ISBN 0–521–38552–0. – ISBN 0–521–38581–4 (pbk.)
1.   Jesus Christ –Teachings.   2. Eschatology – Biblical teaching
3. Bible. N.T. – Criticism, interpretation, etc.   I. Title.
II. Series.
BS2417.E7T54   1990
232 – dc20   89–29714
                                                       CIP

British Library Cataloguing in Publication Data
Tiede, David
Jesus and the future. – (Understanding Jesus today)
I. Jesus Christ
I. Title   II. Series
232

ISBN 0–521–38552–0 hardback
ISBN 0–521–38581–4 paperback

Contents

Introduction: Jesus and History

> He also said to the multitudes, "When you see a cloud rising in the west, you say at once, 'A shower is coming'; and so it happens. And when you see the south wind blowing, you say 'There will be scorching heat'; and it happens. You hypocrites! You know how to interpret the appearance of earth and sky; but why do you not know how to interpret the present time?" (Lk 12:54–6)

The future is big business. It always has been. On New Year's Day, a television news program features an economist with a financial projection, followed by a psychic predicting which movie stars will be divorced. Then a smiling face offers the weather forecast backed up with maps, charts, and numbers. Finally the political commentator ventures that the coming year will be a decisive test for the nation in the areas of tax reform and national defense.

We want to know everything we can about the future, especially our own futures. We are anxious about our health, our children, our finances, the fate of the nation, the poor of the world, and our security in life and in death. We would pay dearly for reliable information, tips, and predictions, eager to find solutions and convinced that ignorance can be very expensive. But who knows what will happen? What kinds of knowledge count? And in which areas? People have all kinds of hunches about the future.

People also have all kinds of opinions about Jesus. Some of these views are well informed, but more often they have little basis in history or the New Testament. And what kinds of knowledge count here? What can be said on the basis of history and the New Testament? Devout believers and skeptics can agree that the story about him is full of details and convictions about the future. But how are they to be understood?

Here is one who was proclaimed as a prophet of God and God's Son on earth, a healer, social critic, and physician of souls. And according to the New Testament, after he was executed he was raised from the dead and declared to be the ruler of heaven and earth. His kingdom is still coming, and he will be the judge of the earth and humanity, dead and alive. What did these powerful affirmations mean to those who knew him and to those who staked their lives on faith in him?

Even now, people who do not accept the Christian faith have often heard these dramatic claims. They may be unsure what to make of Jesus. Christians may also wonder. Many differing claims are made in Jesus' name with conflicting visions of the future.

In one setting, sincere faith and religious hucksterism are melted together in the heat of impassioned threats of Jesus' judgment. Here fearful souls shudder before an angry God. Elsewhere, Jesus is the heavenly messenger of higher knowledge or spiritual wisdom. He declares a new age of self-understanding, far removed from the passions. Are either of these the Jesus of the New Testament? Is it possible to know more about the future he announced? Can careful interpretation shed some light in the midst of such heated confusion?

Jesus and the Future is a tantalizing title. This topic is of broad public interest, and many people hold fervent views. Few are neutral about Jesus, and no one is indifferent about the future, especially their future. It is important, therefore, to remember that this book is one of a series entitled Understanding Jesus Today. This series seeks to assist people to read the

New Testament and understand Jesus in the light of current scholarship.

This book seeks to broaden and clarify the reader's understanding. It does not attack or defend personal convictions. It does not advance a private agenda for the future. But it is also not neutral, because neither history nor the New Testament was ever neutral about Jesus. The story of Jesus is full of convictions about the future. Thus this study describes Jesus' own words and deeds within his times and the religious traditions of Israel. It also gives brief introductions to some of the questions about God and the future that were at stake for the first followers of Jesus, and it demonstrates how early Christian faith in Jesus gave hope for the future in the midst of troubled times.

This is not a book on futurism. It does not pursue the increasingly scientific study of trends and projections, nor does it appeal to Jesus in order to discredit these efforts. The task of building statistical models and making economic and sociological projections has proved its value for business, government, and personal planning. Of course such models of the future are based on assumptions, probabilities, and contingencies. The debate among the futurists is intense. The optimists in technology contend with the environmental pessimists. But this book does not enter that discussion, at least not directly.

On the other hand, the assumptions of some futurists may be challenged by the Jesus traditions of the New Testament. Which factors are decisive in producing the future? Is the future simply a projection of economic indicators? Can it be captured by models of social trends or political ideologies? Perhaps statistical probabilities do not tell the whole human story, past, present, or future. Perhaps history is not merely a "darkling plain" where "ignorant armies clash by night." How shall current discussions accommodate the long-standing convictions of biblical faith? There the meaning and future of human life are caught up in God's purposes and plans. Those who are willing to consider the meaning and morality of the future might well be interested in the Jesus of the New Testament.

This book does not include a list of predictions or prophecies. Some people regard the Bible as a road map of the future that only needs to be decoded, and they pore over Jesus' words and revelations in search of specific modern historical figures and events. Others claim a privileged knowledge of God's plans whether based on their private interpretations of the Bible or their personal religious experiences. This book challenges such usage of the Bible, especially as it is often practiced to manipulate fearful people. But it also affirms the power of religious conviction to name the powers of oppression and to maintain hope in justice and mercy against all appearances.

This is not a devotional book, at least not primarily. The bookshelves are full of volumes in which Jesus is the answer, although the question keeps changing. Jesus has also been brought forward as a spokesman for several visions of the future, some of them full of confidence and others almost eager to declare doom to the planet Earth. But then Jesus himself becomes a serious question. After so many portraits of Jesus have been painted in striking likeness to the artist or the preacher, thinking people begin to object. Which Jesus is this? What was Jesus about in his own time? Why did the Gospels say what they did about him? What vision for the future did he represent to the early Christians? Even modern Christian devotion may be served in the long run if such questions are pursued with vigor and honesty.

This book is concerned with such questions. It informs the reader about current scholarship on Jesus and the New Testament. *Jesus and the Future* is primarily about Jesus and the early Christian testimonies to him. The future under consideration is first the future he prophesied and which they envisioned in his name. This is a study of a particular topic in the New Testament. It highlights crucial passages and shows how to understand what was at stake. It is an introduction to reading the New Testament historically.

Chapter 1, "Jesus and Troubled Times," surveys the common hope of Jesus' people, the Jews or the people of Israel. This hope was grounded in their long history and scriptural heritage, and it was an expectation of God's blessing, salvation, and kingdom. But that history also produced conflicts and divisions in Israel. By the time of Jesus' execution under the Romans in about A.D. 33, several groups and traditions struggled with each other. Each had its views of the past and visions of how God would fulfill Israel's hopes and promises. The future was filled with theological controversy and political consequences.

Chapter 2, "Jesus and the Prophets," focuses on Jesus of Nazareth as he was remembered from his own times. This is a discussion of "the historical Jesus" and what he taught about the future. The Christian sources are more intent on proclaiming him to be the Lord than on recalling the facts of the past, but they still preserve memories of his words and deeds. Jesus' prophetic role and his confidence of the depth of God's gracious ways still leave their mark on the Christian stories.

Chapter 3, "Jesus and the Kingdom," deals with Jesus as he was proclaimed to be the Messiah and Lord in the years of the early Christian movement. This is a discussion of "the Christ of faith" and how the stories were told and the Gospels were written to proclaim God's judgment and hope in Jesus' name. The faith of the early Christians affirmed that Jesus brought God's heavenly Reign to earth and authorized them to announce it. Christian hope for the future made their present meaningful.

Chapter 4, "Jesus and the End," presents Jesus as he was envisioned in the Revelation to John. This is a discussion of hope in Christ's justice and mercy. In the face of cruel threats, the remedy of salvation is severe. But God has not destined the world for ultimate destruction. The "apocalypse" or "revelation" is a vision of God's final renewal and restoration of the earth.

Reading the New Testament historically, therefore, proves to be an introduction to the hopes of Israel in the Roman era, the message of Jesus, the proclamation of the early Christians, and the adamant faith of those who appeared to have no future. This also proves to be a theological reading because both Jesus and his followers believed God to be the Lord of history. In the New Testament, it is not possible to know the future without understanding what is going on between God and humanity in the present.

Readers need to consider the relevance of these testimonies to their sense of the future and the present. Those who merely want to predict what is going to happen may be disappointed to discover how open the future was for Jesus and his followers. But the task of understanding Jesus today requires knowledge of the past. Such understanding also produces an appreciation of the ways that faith in God was shaped in human experience, and it illumines how that faith also shaped the future. The story of Jesus is an assurance of hope for the future of the world, but it is not a naive optimism. It was forged in the fires of conflict with powers and dominions that seemed to rob the future of hope.

Chapter 1

Jesus and Troubled Times

Crucified under Pontius Pilate

So they took Jesus, and he went out, bearing his own cross, to the place called the place of the skull, which is called in Hebrew Golgotha. There they crucified him, and with him two others, one on either side, and Jesus between them. Pilate also wrote a title and put it on the cross; it read, "Jesus of Nazareth, the King of the Jews." (Jn 19:17–19)

The story of Jesus and the future must begin in the past, and it must begin at his death. This is not the fabled past of "once upon a time," which could only yield a fictional future. This is the flesh-and-blood past in which crucifixion was a cruel form of public execution generally reserved for slaves and enemies of the Roman order. It is an era in history when the Roman legions had occupied Palestine for almost a century, and only the Senate and emperor in Rome could declare someone to be "King of the Jews." It is during the decade (A.D. 26–36) when Pontius Pilate was the governor, charged with keeping the peace in a region that was known to be a seedbed of trouble. The title he placed over Jesus' head was not a confession of faith. It was a bitter warning to all Judea against any dreams of future revolt.

Those facts of history were already more than bare facts. They were filled with interpretation and meaning. Consider the scene from Pilate's point of view. This was not a casual murder in a dark alley, nor a human sacrifice to appease the gods. It was an authorized execution carried out by troops under his command, and it was meant to send a message. A dead "King of the Jews" would offer no future. The authority and the future lay with Roman destiny.

Most of the discussion of Jesus and the future will focus on Jesus as one who interpreted and enacted the hope and faith of Israel. His vision of the future was clearly controversial among his own people. But the Romans also had convictions about history and hopes for the future, and they certainly were not focused on Jewish prophets or the God of Israel. Their poets, historians, and prophets declared the Roman Peace or the Peace of Caesar Augustus to be a sacred trust. The ideal of security was to be defended at all costs, and its traits were well known in their heritage:

. . . the official religion of worship and divination, executive authority, senatorial influence, statute and customary law, the popular courts and magisterial jurisdiction, good faith, the provinces and allies, imperial prestige, military and financial strength. (Cicero, "Pro Sestio," 45–46)

This is a worldview of order. The power of the state is to be maintained and justified as the will of the gods. It is a concept of history that made sense to those who were running the world. Every empire has such claims to legitimacy, and ancient kingdoms were especially religious in their claims. Their politics were always "theocratic," at least in their claims of divine favor or authority. Their subject nations were seldom consulted.

Pilate probably did not consider Jesus to be an imposing threat to the grand Roman vision of a golden age of peace and prosperity. He may have regarded the controversy surrounding Jesus as merely another local disturbance, a Jewish dispute to be settled quickly in the midst of a religious holiday. Nevertheless, Pilate was administering policies that were full of political and religious convictions, and he was wrapped in the cloak of Roman authority as a governor. He would not have appreciated the implied threat that he would not be "Caesar's friend" if he did not execute Jesus (Jn 19:12). His verdict and charge intended to crush any hopes or dreams of the future associated with Jesus.

Of course the New Testament story was not told from Pilate's point of view nor from the perspective of the Temple leaders who were in close collaboration with the Roman rule. The meaning of the execution was not dictated by Pilate or the religious rulers who opposed Jesus. Jesus' followers declared an alternative theology of history and the future. Every surviving first-century version announces that Jesus was raised from the dead. God had vindicated Jesus. "God has made him Lord and Messiah," they said, "this Jesus whom you crucified" (Acts 2:36). Or as Paul stated it, "We impart a secret and hidden wisdom of God, which God decreed before the ages for our glorification. None of the rulers of this age understood this; for if they had, they would not have crucified the Lord of glory" (1 Cor 2:7–8).

The early Christians understood the facts and the future quite differently from Pilate. They knew that they were telling the story from the underside of history. They were persuaded that Jesus truly was "The King of the Jews." God's will and reign were at work in Jesus, and Jesus was now established as the ultimate ruler of heaven and earth. "Jesus is Lord!" was their conviction about God and the world, and "O Lord come!" was their hope for the future.

Therefore our topic is a historical one, in at least two senses. First, the history of his times are crucial to understanding both Jesus and the future he declared. Jesus did not appear in a vacuum. He was surrounded by conflicts in his social, political, and religious culture, and he was executed as a royal pretender. That historical past is central to what he meant. Pontius Pilate and the apostle Paul could have agreed that Jesus was executed in a particular time and place. Perhaps they would have agreed that it was a test of whose gods were ultimate. It might even be possible for a later Roman governor to understand that Jesus was thought to be alive (see Acts 25:13–22). But the Romans and religious leaders in occupied Palestine could not accept the claims made in his name without changing their whole understanding of the world.

Thus ours is also a historical subject in a second sense in that it is a proposal about the meaning of history. Jesus makes sense only when he is seen within the heritage of Israel. The historical facts are indispensable, but the meaning of those facts is even more crucial. The issue is more "What is going on in history?" than simply "What happened?" The conflict that led to Jesus' death was about the Kingdom of God or how God has chosen to rule in the world. In the grand sweep of history, this was a conflict with the Roman order, but first of all Jesus posed a challenge to Israel and its leaders.

To understand the future Jesus proclaimed, it is necessary to understand why existing systems of authority felt threatened by him. It is necessary to recall the moral and religious myths and symbols by which the world lived and legitimated itself. Jesus did not simply predict the future. He declared the coming of God's Reign in terms that redefined the meaning of the present and future.

The story of Jesus and the future begins with the public event of his execution. The Romans sought to put an end to Jesus and the Kingdom of God he proclaimed, but his followers regarded his death as crucial to the "hidden wisdom of God," which the "rulers of this age" did not understand. This story then circles back into the history of the Scriptures of Israel, returns to Jesus, and then out into the proclamation of the Christ and his kingdom in the following decades. The Christian story is a distinctive interpretation of the hope of Israel. It is filled with the heritage of Israel's scriptural faith and played out against the backdrop of world history. It is a declaration of the will and plan of God in the midst of human affairs.

In Order That the Scripture May Be Fulfilled

So all the generations from Abraham to David were fourteen generations, and from David to the deportation to Babylon fourteen generations, and from the deportation to Babylon to the Christ fourteen generations. (Mt 1:17)

Jesus had a historical past. It was Israel's past, variously told to reach back to King David, Father Abraham, and Mother Sarah, or to the distant recesses of Noah before the Flood or Adam and Eve at the Creation. Matthew's genealogy of Jesus begins with Abraham (1:1–16) whereas Luke traces his ancestry to Adam, the son of God (3:23–38). Jesus is never quoted as commenting extensively on this history. In John's Gospel, Jesus emphasizes that he is not merely a product of the past (8:48–59), but he always identified Israel and its Scriptures as the primary arena where God's Reign and word were revealed. Both Jesus and his disciples were thoroughly at home in Israel's faith and heritage.

The sacred institutions or marks of that heritage were the Torah and the Temple, the Scriptures of Israel and the house of God in Jerusalem. The land was also a sacred trust, given by God to the people of Israel, and the local synagogue was the house of prayer and study throughout the many lands where Jews lived. But Israel's security and blessing lay in God's determined will in the Scriptures and sheltering presence in the Temple.

Neither Jesus nor his contemporaries possessed a Bible, as modern people own books, or even an "Old Testament" in the form of one volume. The "scriptures" were collections of scrolls or books, including the Torah or five scrolls of Moses, the prophets, and the Psalms with various other "writings." All communities did not possess all the same writings, and their

handwritten copies were far from standardized. The line between "Holy Book" and "sacred tradition" was not drawn so
sharply in Jesus' world. The texts were read aloud in the community, and the commentary could precede, follow, or accompany
the reading.

The Scriptures and the proclaimed word of God were the
primary means of revelation in Jesus' world. In the synagogues
of Galilee, Judea, and beyond, scriptural interpretation was pursued with discipline and passion. Here the sacred heritage was
probed in order to conform belief and practice to the will of
God. Here also the disputes with the scribes and Pharisees
could reach white heat as differences of interpretation displayed competing convictions. The symbolic construction of
the universe was at stake, and the Scriptures were both the
common ground and the battleground. "What is written in the
law?", Jesus asks the interpreter in Luke 10:26, and "How do
you read?" The first question appeals to the text that unites
Israel and the second calls for its decisive meaning.

Other Jewish groups such as the Sadducees and high priests
were more oriented to the Temple with its priesthood and sacrifices. The Temple was far more than a building. Like the
Scriptures, it was a sacral institution, a common ground for
Israel's identity and a battleground for alternative traditions.
People who had never been there could have strong opinions
about its priests and practices, just as people who had not read
the Scriptures could argue or die for their holiness or inspiration. The Temple was the house where God's hovering presence in the holy sanctuary protected Israel. The sacred canopy
could be rent only if God abandoned the Temple and the city.
Those who were critical of the Temple and its priesthood
might announce its doom in a prophetic call for repentance,
but no one could regard its fate lightly.

The Pharisees and the Christians also revered the Temple,
but they were more centered in the synagogue with its scrip-

tural and scribal practices. It is not an accident that the Pharisees and Christians were able to survive the destruction of the Temple and Jerusalem as vigorous forms of the faith of Israel when the Sadducees, Herodians, and high priestly parties disappeared. On a few occasions, the New Testament even offers glimpses of the Christians and the Pharisees closing ranks against the intimidating power of the Temple leadership (see Mk 12:18–34; Lk 20:27–40; Mt 22:23–40; Acts 23:6–10).

The passage from Matthew 1:17 cited at the beginning of this section demonstrates the continuing interest of the Christian scribal tradition in the interpretation of Israel's history. The three cycles of fourteen generations from Abraham to David to the Exile to the Christ offer a schema of God's architecture of history. Of course if the past displays such order for those who know its fulfillment in Jesus, the future must also lie in God's hands. But Matthew's schema also highlights three of the most formative factors of Israel's scriptural understanding of history: the call of Abraham, the kingdom of David, and the Babylonian Exile. The stories of Moses and the Exodus are noticeably absent from this scheme. Still, Matthew's timeline is a helpful memory device for recalling the past Jesus shared with Israel.

Abraham		David	Exile	Jesus
	(Moses)	1000 B.C.	587 B.C.	4 B.C.

Abraham lies in the distant past, but his importance is not confined there. He and Sarah bear the child of promise, and he is the father of many nations who trusted God when the future of his family appeared lost. The narratives of Genesis 12–25 form the identity of the children of Abraham around God's promises of children, land, and nation. These stories further bond the family to God through the covenant of circumcision.

The future is assured through faithfulness to God, and God has blessed Abraham in order to bring blessing to all the families of the earth (Gn 12:3). God has chosen him "that he may charge his children and his household after him to keep the way of the Lord by doing righteousness and justice; so that the Lord may bring to Abraham what he has promised him" (Gn 18:19). Israel's theology of history is anchored in this dynamic relationship between God and the people of the promise.

David's kingdom was remembered to follow Moses and the Exodus by a few centuries. This was the era of the consolidation of the nation from a loose confederation of tribes, and it was the golden age of the kingdom of Judah. The memory, however, may have been as important as the fact because it was charged with both identity and future. David's kingdom was God's will and reign, and God had promised David, "I will raise up your offspring after you, who shall come forth from your body, and I will establish his kingdom. He shall build a house for my name, and I will establish the throne of his kingdom forever. I will be his father, and he shall be my son" (2 Sm 7:12–14).

The Exile, which began in 597–587 B.C., was the crucible in which Israel's understanding of history was decisively forged. Other ancient religious traditions also spoke of divine favor on certain tribes and families. Oriental traditions of kingship often included assurances of eternal legitimacy and prosperity. Official books and declarations supported the rulers and priests. Generally such narratives were court histories. They were commissioned by the regime in power to validate the status quo as divinely established forever.

But Israel collected these ancestral stories and composed them into the books of Moses after being conquered by the neo-Babylonian empire. The sources included traditions from the glorious reign of the Davidic kings, but Israel's history could not claim that they and their God had always triumphed against the kingdoms of the earth. When the promises of God appeared to have failed or other gods seemed to have prevailed, then Israel's history was written. When the Temple lay in ruins, the priests in exile envisioned a restoration of the sacrifices. Confident of God's promises to Abraham, Moses, and David, they interpreted their present as a time of God's judgment, and they focused their faith on the future.

The scribes in the Babylonian Exile prepared new editions of the traditions of the patriarchs, the history of the Exodus, and the oracles of the prophets. In this restatement of the tradition, Moses stood forward as a prophet, predicting at the end of his life that they would be "a perverse generation, children in whom there is no faithfulness" (Dt 31–4).

Divine judgment and blessing were both promised in Israel's Scriptures, and the problem of God's justice resisted simplistic solutions. The future would never be merely the legitimation of the status quo. In the Psalms, Lamentations, Jeremiah, Isaiah, and Job's debates with his counselors, Israel rehearsed its complex faith that God is at work in history. God is contending with a willful humanity. Israel has made the terrible mistake of presuming on God's goodwill. The only thing worse is the error of Israel's enemies, who assume that Israel's God is powerless to help them.

Israel saw God's reign of righteousness being tested in history. God might even have destroyed sinful Israel except for the false pride and idolatry of its adversaries (Dt 32:26–43; Is 40–55). Israel's hope for the future is finally grounded in the conviction that God is God. "Behold, I have refined you, but not like silver; I have tried you in the furnace of affliction. For my own sake, for my own sake, I do it, for how should my name be profaned? My glory I will not give to another" (Is 48:10–11).

This scriptural legacy from the Exile defined Israel's distinctive understanding of history and the future. God's reign of righteousness had not failed although the kingdom of David had been conquered. The future still belonged to the faithful because God is faithful and God is God. The later prophecies of Isaiah 40–66, Ezekiel 33–48, and Zechariah 9–14 were again full of promises of restoration, but these promises were expressions of hope more than of fact. The process of return and rebuilding of Jerusalem began in the later part of that century (538–515 B.C.), but Israel would remain scattered in Babylon, Egypt, and Asia Minor. Even after many people returned to Judea in subsequent generations, the dream of the restoration of the kingdom was largely unfulfilled. This hope lay at the heart of Israel's identity, but it was open to many interpretations.

The Kingdom Restored

After this I saw in the night visions, and behold, a fourth beast, terrible and dreadful and exceedingly strong; and it had great iron teeth; it devoured and broke in pieces, and stamped the residue with its feet. It was different from all the beasts that were before it; and it had ten horns. I considered the horns and behold, there come up among them another horn, a little one, before which three of the first horns were plucked up by the roots; and behold in this horn were eyes like the eyes of a man, and a mouth speaking great things. . . . As I looked this horn made war with the saints, and prevailed over them, until the Ancient of Days came, and judgment was given for the saints of the Most High, and the time came when the saints received the kingdom. (Dn 7:7–8, 21–2).

The larger political arena was altered again when Alexander the Great conquered the region. His successors ruled Palestine from 323 to 167 B.C., with a change in overlords from the Greeks in Egypt to the Greeks in the East occurring in 200 B.C. Many prominent Jews, including the priestly families, found the Greek era quite comfortable. There was no great need to transform the world. The Temple leadership even raised the taxes for the Greeks and received a commission for their efforts. They certainly had no need for trouble. Talk of reform or restoration held little promise for them, and they had a century and a half to make the Temple a model of success in the Greek world. The Temple was a center of economic exchange as well as the place of Jewish prayers and sacrifices.

But a great crisis lay ahead in the second century B.C. The Greek ruler Antiochus IV (Epiphanes) and the aristocratic Jerusalem priests began to buy and sell the high priesthood. It was a powerful office, after all, and the Greeks were accustomed to controlling Hellenistic temples with favors, friendship, and demands of tribute. In the ancient world where all politics were thoroughly religious, rulers often assumed that all religion was also thoroughly political. Both the Greeks and the Hellenized Jewish priests underestimated the piety of the people.

An internal revolt among the Jerusalem priests prompted Antiochus to raid the Temple treasury and abolish local practice. In 167 B.C., he seized the Temple and dedicated it to Dionysius. He established sacrifices that were an insult to the Jews and banned the practice of circumcision, on pain of death. It was a heavy-handed act by all standards. He was determined to exert absolute control over this vassal state on the frontier with Egypt. He also needed the funds from the treasury. Antiochus was accustomed to the Hellenized high priests, and he expected to establish an even more "enlightened" Greek leadership in a temple more fitting to his image of himself as virtually divine. He was not prepared for the depth of the reaction.

For the faithful in Israel, this was "the abomination that makes desolate," and Antiochus was the "little horn" of the great Greek beast "speaking great things." Many people viewed the Greek conquest as God's judgment on a sinful priesthood. The Book of Daniel interpreted this history in the form of a "revelation" or an "apocalypse" where finally the powers of heaven were to be revealed against such blasphemy. The desecration by Antiochus finally threatened the end of history itself because it challenged God's Reign with a "merely human" authority. It assaulted God's dominion in Israel in the name of the idols of Greek religion as promoted by a pretentious ruler. Whatever role the Greeks played in God's plan in history, they could not supplant God. The future belonged to God alone, and Israel could not accommodate Antiochus' program without faithlessness or apostasy. Thus Daniel sorted out the severe options that confronted Israel:

He shall seduce with flattery those who violate the covenant; but the people who know their God shall stand firm and take action. And those among the people who are wise shall make many understand, though they shall fall by sword and flame, by captivity and plunder for some days. (Dn 11:29–35)

The very fabric of the meaning of history and the future was threatened. The faith and identity of Israel were at stake. This was holy war, and its captain, Judas Maccabeus, led the Hasmonean family into power as they drove out the Greeks. They declared that the God of Israel was pitted against the gods of the Gentiles, and the decisions of war were legitimated with sacred ritual:

They fasted that day, put on sackcloth and sprinkled ashes on their heads, and rent their clothes. And they opened the book of the law to inquire into those matters about which the Gentiles were consulting the images of their idols. They also brought the garments of the priesthood and the first fruits and the tithes, and they stirred up the Nazirites who had completed their days; and they cried aloud to heaven. (1 Mc 3:47–50)

Their court histories could claim that within two years they had restored "blameless priests," purified the Temple in Jerusalem, rekindled the sacred flame, and collected all the books (1 Mc 4:36–61; 2 Mc 2 and 10). When the Hasmoneans established themselves as the high priests and kings of Israel, they were the first Jewish kings since David's line ended in exile. They declared, "It is God who has saved all his people, and has returned the inheritance to all, and the kingship and priest-hood and consecration, as he promised through the law" (2 Mc 2:17).

Their victory was wrapped in the sacred cloth of scriptural history and understood as a fulfillment of God's promised judgment and salvation, and the Temple was the crucial sign of the state of God's relationship to Israel:

The Lord did not choose the nation for the sake of the holy place, but the place for the sake of the nation. Therefore the place itself shared in the misfortunes that befell the nation and afterward participated in its benefits; and what was forsaken in the wrath of the Almighty was restored again in all its glory when the great Lord became reconciled. (2 Mc 5:19–20)

Throughout the next century, the Hasmoneans were able to keep the Greek kingdoms to the south and the east at bay, often by paying tribute and by alliances with Rome in the west. In a carefully balanced power vacuum maintained by Rome, Israel's priest-kings ran a successful oriental monarchy. They reestablished the boundaries of David's realm, and they compelled allegiance in the conquered regions of Galilee and Idumea to the Judean state, to its Temple, and even to the practice of circumcision. But this was not the restoration of the kingdom that many in Israel had in mind. For those who were alienated from the kingdom of the Hasmoneans, foreign domination may have been easier to accept than their rule in God's name.

If Israel's complex historical faith was forged in the fires of the Exile, as I have suggested, it was tried in the chill waters of the Hasmonean kingdom, and severely fractured. The hope of a genuine theocracy in which God's righteous rule is exercised by legitimate kings and priests could unite a scattered people. It could even rally a revolution against the Greeks.

But this hope was never a simple ideology supported by a unified community. Differing groups clung to alternative visions of how God rules the world and how God's people should be faithful. They probably even read different scriptures and identified more closely with different practices and institutions. The cracks in the unity of Israel were evident early, and they would develop into serious divisions. The hope for the restoration of the kingdom gave power to transform the world the Greeks sought to establish. It did not easily legitimate the order the Hasmoneans sought to perpetuate.

First it was "the pious ones" or "the Hasideans" who "were seeking righteousness and justice" and "went down to the wilderness to dwell there." Some of them refused to fight on the Sabbath, preferring to "die in our innocence," passively resisting breaking the law rather than fighting in the same manner as the Greeks (1 Mc 1:62–3; 2:29–48). The restoration of the kingdom that they envisioned did not allow the kind of political compromises the Hasmoneans found necessary.

Then a covenant community withdrew to the Qumran region of the Dead Sea with their priests and scribes. For over two centuries until the Romans destroyed them, they pursued a separate life and pored over their scrolls. They complained bitterly about "the seekers of smooth things" in Jerusalem, and they dreamed of divine intervention. They apparently saw the Hasmonean high priest named Simon as an adversary of their leader, the Righteous Teacher.

Their vision of the future included a holy war fought by the heavenly armies against the existing priests and their gentile allies. They looked for a new temple led by their divinely legitimate priests. In the meantime, "for as long as the dominion of Satan endures," they were ordered "according to the everlasting design" with the priests "ranked one after another according to the perfection of their spirit; then the Levites; and thirdly all the people one after another, in their Thousands, Hundreds, Fifties, and Tens, that every Israelite may know his place in the Community of God" (Community Rule 2.19–23).

Such alienation was probably extreme, but it was an aggressive program of "righteousness" and "faithfulness" that stood against the theocracy in Jerusalem. At Qumran, the high priest in Jerusalem, Simon, was called "the wicked priest," but the official Hasmonean history insisted that

the people saw Simon's faithfulness . . . and they made him their leader and high priest because he had done all these things and because of the justice and loyalty which he had maintained toward his nation.

Even the Hasmonean history conceded that the Greek king Demetrius was the one who "confirmed him in the high priesthood" after he saw that "the Romans had received the envoys of Simon with honor." The Hasmoneans were very candid in identifying the support of foreign rulers for their priestly kingdom. Furthermore, once Simon was clothed in purple and wearing gold, he silenced dissent: "None of the people or priests shall be permitted to nullify any of these decisions or to oppose what he says, or to convene an assembly in the country without his permission" (1 Mc 14:35–49).

The Pharisees also took exception to the despotism of the Hasmoneans, especially to the high priesthood of Simon's grandson, who bore the Greek name Alexander Jannaeus. He was a great success at expanding the kingdom, but his reputation grew for cruelty and abuse of his high priestly duties. The Jewish historian Josephus, who favored the Pharisees, later reported that they finally pelted him with the ripe fruit of a harvest festival in protest.

The Pharisees' program of righteousness and faithfulness had provoked them to acts of public protest over the observances of the Temple ritual. For them, these matters could not be separated into either "religion" or "politics." The future of Israel rested with obedience to divine commands. The safety of the nation was at stake in the Temple liturgy. According to Josephus, civil war soon broke out, and Alexander Jannaeus crushed it with intense cruelty: "While he feasted with his concubines in a conspicuous place, he ordered some eight hundred of the Jews to be crucified, and slaughtered their children and wives before the eyes of the still living wretches" (*Antiquities* 13.372, 380).

The century of the Hasmonean kingdom ended in 63 B.C. when the Roman general Pompey besieged Jerusalem and desecrated the Temple by marching into the holy sanctuary. It was the second time since the Exile that gentile armies had defiled the Temple, but now the alien entered the city on the invitation of one of two Hasmoneans who claimed the high priesthood. The mantle of legitimacy was in tatters. The lament went up to God, but the Romans were not going to leave. It appeared to some to be God's judgment on Israel:

Foreign nations went up to thine altar,
In pride they trampled it with their sandals;
Because the sons of Jerusalem had defiled the sanctuary of the Lord,
Had profaned the offering to God with lawless deeds. (Pss Sol 2.2–3)

The Birth of the Messiah

Now when Jesus was born in Bethlehem of Judea in the days of Herod the king, behold, wise men from the East came to Jerusalem, saying, "Where is he who has been born king of the Jews? For we have seen his star in the East, and have come to worship him." When Herod, the king heard this, he was troubled, and all Jerusalem with him. (Mt 2:1–3)
In those days a decree went out from Caesar Augustus that all the world should be enrolled. This was the first enrollment, when Quirinius was governor of Syria. And all went to be enrolled, each to his own city. . . . And the angel said to them, "Be not afraid; for behold, I bring you good news of a great joy which will come to all the people; for to you is born this day in the city of David a Savior, who is Christ the Lord." (Lk 2:1–2, 10–11)

This historical review that began with Jesus' crucifixion now returns to the era of his birth. The arrival of Pompey and defiling of the Temple marked the beginning of Roman rule in Palestine. It occurred about sixty years before Jesus was born and almost a century before he was executed by Pilate. The following chapters will highlight the era of Jesus, the times in which the gospel traditions were developed, and the critical moment of the Revelation to John. All of these lie within the first century as well as within the era of Roman rule. A timeline may again offer some perspective.

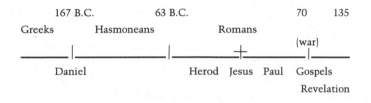

This chart places Jesus in the midst of the major public crises of Judean history of the era, with each date marking a conquest or defilement of the Temple: first the Greek desecration under Antiochus Epiphanes in 167 B.C., then three Roman assaults: The first is Pompey's conquest and defilement in 63 B.C., the second is the siege and destruction of the city by Titus in 70 A.D., and the last is the conquest by Hadrian (135) when the Temple site was finally plowed and perhaps dedicated as a shrine to Jupiter.

In this historical context, Jesus spoke of the present and the future, and the early Christians later recited his words and envisioned his revelation. Of course any simplified chart will omit far more than it will include of the living and meaning of an era. Many other events occurred in these three hundred years beyond these national calamities, and other aspects of personal and public life will be mentioned in the following chapters. But the dates of the Temple calamities are more than chronological benchmarks because the Temple was so central to Israel's history and future. For the followers of Jesus, the fate of the Temple was tied directly to his mission to Israel and reign as Messiah.

Two other historical figures must be discussed briefly, Caesar Augustus and Herod the Great. Not only are both of them mentioned in the New Testament accounts of Jesus' birth, but they are figures who cast long shadows over Jewish and Roman history in the first century. The former is the great Roman emperor who inaugurated the golden age of peace and prosperity, and the latter is the "King of the Jews" whose reign was a great success and a bitter disappointment for the faithful in Israel.

Of course Augustus stepped into the second act of the drama of Jewish history under Rome. When Pompey arrived earlier in Syria (63 B.C.), Israel's future was already tied to Rome. Then civil war broke out among Julius Caesar, Pompey, Mark Antony, and Octavian (later called Augustus), and the Jews were embroiled in the struggle. But Jewish efforts to reestablish independence in the midst of such instability proved futile. Local leaders and institutions were compelled to take sides, first with a renewed Greek kingdom of Egypt until Antony and Cleopatra ended their rule and lives in suicide. Then Augustus' rule was the future, and Herod the Great was his local king.

Octavian's reign as Caesar Augustus extended from 27 B.C. to 14 A.D. He was able to put an end to rebellions and administer the empire in good order. The poets, historians, and official proclamations of Rome declared him to be the savior and benefactor sent by the gods. His birthday was declared to be the beginning of a new era for all humanity. One famous (and wordy) decree from the eastern provinces at midcareer announced:

Whereas,
Providence that orders all our lives has in her display of concern and generosity in our behalf adorned our lives with the highest good: Augustus, whom she has filled with virtue for the benefit of human-

ity . . . a Savior who has made war to cease and who shall put everything in peaceful order; And whereas,

Caesar transcended the expectations of all . . . with the result that
the birthday of our God signaled the beginning of the Good News for
the world because of him; And whereas,

after the assembly of Asia decreed . . . that a crown be awarded to
the person who came up with the best proposal for honoring our
God . . . And whereas,

the proconsul Paul Fabius Maximus, benefactor of the province . . .
has discovered a way to honor Augustus that was hitherto unknown
among the Greeks, namely to reckon time from the date of his
nativity; It shall be proclaimed:

Asia crowns Paullus Fabius Maximus for his most pious proposal of
honors for Caesar. (*First Decree of Asian League* 30–76)

This proclamation is datable to a few years before the birth of
Jesus. It is a fascinating display of public piety that seeks to
gain favor for the region in Caesar's eyes at the same time that
it announces political and religious fidelity. It is also remarkable because it suggests that the whole calendar should count
the years from Caesar's birth. Changing the calendar was no
small matter, especially in the ancient world. These are the
very frameworks of life, full of divine threat and promise. The
proposal to redate all time from the nativity of the "Savior" is,
therefore, a statement about the meaning of history and the
future, whether that is Augustus or Jesus.

The Jews also benefited from a benevolent policy in Augustus' reign. Later Jewish authors would appeal to Augustus
and to Julius Caesar before him to defend their special convictions and practices. Philo, a Jewish philosopher in Alexandria,
waxed eloquent in his praise:

Again consider him who in all the virtues transcended human nature,
who on account of the vastness of his imperial sovereignty as well as
nobility of character was the first to bear the name of the August or
Venerable . . . Augustus whom men fitly call the averter of evil. This
is the Caesar who calmed the torrential storms on every side, who
healed the pestilences common to Greeks and barbarians . . . who led

disorder into order and brought gentle manners and harmony . . . the firsthand the greatest and the common benefactor in that he displaced the rule of many and committed the ship of the commonwealth to be steered by a single pilot, that is himself, a marvelous master of the science of government. (*Embassy to Gaius* 143–8)

Such praise is rather standard fare in the first century, and its extravagance was part of the style. Still, Philo was a Jewish author joining the acclaim of Augustus as one who "transcended human nature," calming storms and healing diseases. Philo's point was to chide a later Roman emperor, Gaius Caligula, who abused his authority and claimed divine honors for himself. Thus Philo insisted that the great Augustus was regarded as heaven sent because he was such a benefactor and savior and not a tyrant. His grace toward the Jews and respect of the Temple fit that role. And because Augustus did not insist on being worshiped like a god, the Jews could join the chorus of those who recognized God's salvation in his reign.

Herod the Great had been established in Palestinian politics before Augustus became emperor, and he was able to survive the Roman civil war. The Romans named him "The King of the Jews" first as an ally of Antony and later reconfirmed by Augustus and the Roman Senate. His reign lasted from 31 to 4 B.C. in the face of great political complexity. He was an Idumean by birth and thus suspected by many Judeans as an alien king. He was a great success in military and administrative ventures, and he built impressive Hellenistic cities.

He also began an ambitious rebuilding of the Temple that was still not complete when the Romans destroyed it seventy-five years after he died. His taxes matched his projects in grandeur. In order to deal with the opposition that arose from the Hasmonean family, he arranged the assassination of the last of the high priests from the line, and he married into it to legitimize his own reign and progeny. But the palace intrigues continued, and so did his paranoia.

In his last years, Herod was renowned for cruelty. He executed his own children at the thought that they might displace him from his throne or even that they might rejoice at his death. He also had erected a golden eagle on the rebuilt Temple, but this image was attacked by forty young men with hatchets who had been stirred with religious zeal by their teachers. In Josephus' lurid account of his end, Herod orders these men to be executed at the moment he dies, saying to his sister,

"I know that the Jews will celebrate my death by a festival; yet I can obtain a vicarious mourning and a magnificent funeral, if you consent to follow my instructions. You know these men here in custody; the moment I expire have them surrounded by the soldiers and massacred; so shall all Judea and every household weep for me, whether they will or no." (*War* 1.660)

Matthew's Gospel (2:16–19) also reports that this Herod is the one who ordered the slaughter of all male children under two years of age in the region of Bethlehem. Even at the end of his life, he could not allow a Davidic "King of the Jews" to emerge. It is difficult to verify the historical accuracy of these terrible stories of Herod's last years, but the consistency of the picture is fascinating. Herod the Great, the King of the Jews, was hated and feared. He was admired for his skill as leader, architect, and oriental ruler, and he had a kingdom almost as great as that of David a thousand years before or that of the Hasmoneans a century earlier. He even had a temple more glorious than that of Solomon. But he was still a client king of the Roman order. And even if this was the golden age of Caesar Augustus, it was not the fulfillment of God's promises to Abraham or David.

Looking for the Consolation of Israel

Behold, this child is set for the fall and rising of many in Israel and for a sign that is spoken against (and a sword will pierce through your own soul also), that thoughts out of many hearts may be revealed. (Lk 2:34b–35)

By the time of Jesus, Israel's faith in God was filled with the scriptural refrains of hope for "restoration of the kingdom," "the redemption of Jerusalem," "the consolation of Israel," and the coming of "the kingdom of God" in righteousness and mercy. The agent of this salvation was variously identified as "the Son of man," "the prophet like Moses," "Elijah," "the Son of God," or "the Messiah," and each of these titles (among others) gathered different specific expectations for various groups of people.

That was exactly the problem. The common faith was far from uniform. It admitted a wide variety of concepts of how God's Reign would be established on earth and how God's will would be accomplished. Differing communities each nurtured particular and competitive visions of the promised future.

The Herodians and high priests in the era of Pilate were committed to the Temple, its sanctity, and its treasury. The Sadducees probably shared their investment in the centrality of the Temple. This was the institution that the Romans allowed to sustain the religious and national heritage. It had a court system, an economic basis and coinage all its own, and a legislative role at least with its loyal supporters. The high priests were appointed by the Roman governors, and the sacred garments were occasionally impounded by the Romans to regulate the festivals. The priests were required to offer daily sacrifices on behalf of the emperor, and no one would claim that the Temple or its leadership was anything but loyal to Rome. But that was reality, and the Herodians, high priests, and Sadducees were relatively prosperous.

It is common for interpreters to be critical of these Temple groups or to dismiss them as hypocritical aristocrats. The New Testament is harsh on them, and so are the traditions of the rabbis and the books from Qumran. Modern religious, cultural, and ideological biases against the upper classes or economically advantaged often reinforce those ancient criticisms. Furthermore, almost nothing survives from their own testimony. Once the Temple was gone, their voice fell silent in history. Josephus tells several fascinating stories of the heroic efforts the Herodians and the Temple leadership made to preserve its sanctity against desecration by Roman officials such as Pilate or Caligula and against plunder by the masses. But Josephus wore his own aristocratic loyalties very publically.

It is important to say, however, that these Temple leadership groups were not all evil or self-serving. They had a worship tradition that they believed sustained the presence of God in the midst of Israel. Many people also trusted the sanctity of the Temple and its practices, and those who cooperated with Rome justified their policies on the basis of protecting the Temple. They knew that the Romans had little understanding and less genuine respect for their religious convictions or practices. They had to be accommodating where they could be and firm when that was required.

Even their concern for preserving the nation into the future was anchored in protecting the Temple. The practice of righteousness was the faithful observance of the worship of Israel. This is how the Reign of God was manifest in Israel at that time, without any fantasies about the future. According to the Gospel of John, some of them feared Jesus' popularity because, "If we let him go on thus, every one will believe in him, and the Romans will come and destroy both our holy place and our nation" (11:48). Some of them eventually died in the midst of the sacrifices when the Romans conquered the Temple. Both their religious convictions and their vested interests affected their vision of the future.

The sectarians in the wilderness were alienated from this vision of the future, as noted earlier in the discussion on Qumran. They could afford to be purists, standing aloof from the politics and economics of the Temple. Their program of righteousness and faithfulness would extend to every aspect of community life and bodily function. The future lay with the faithful, that is, the observant who would be ready for God's new order free from the taint of the ways and idols of the Gentiles.

Their wilderness also hosted another kind of popular prophets and revolutionaries. Today they might well be identified as guerrilla fighters, but Josephus and the Romans called them "bandits" or "brigands." Now and again the Romans would mount a raid on one of these groups.

According to Josephus, early in the first century Judas the Galilean "incited his countrymen to revolt, upbraiding them as cowards for consenting to pay tribute to the Romans and tolerating mortal masters, after having God for their lord" (*War* 2.118).

Another "prophet" named Theudas gathered a large following with promises that the Jordan River would part before them. This was apparently a symbol of a reconquest of the land with God's help just as Joshua had "passed over the Jordan" to conquer the land long ago (Jos 3). The Romans took it seriously. They attacked and killed many, and they cut off Theudas' head and brought it back to Jerusalem (*Antiquities* 20.98). Those who envisioned a future in which God would lead a rebellion to free the land from Roman occupation met with harsh treatment.

The Pharisees, meanwhile, appear to have participated in the Temple, but they stood apart from the high priests. Again the first-century sources are limited. Much of the datable information comes from Josephus and the New Testament, and the rabbinic sources that speak for the Pharisees were written later. The severe words in the New Testament about the Pharisees simply indicate again that the tensions between differing Jewish groups could be intense. The meaning and hope of the scriptural faith were at stake.

Above all, the Pharisees had become a reform movement in

Israel, focused on the observance of the Law of Moses. The future of Israel lay with faithfulness to Torah, with observance of the practices and rituals in all of life. The study and interpretation of the Scriptures occurred everywhere, not merely in the Temple in Jerusalem. In Babylon, Asia Minor, Rome, Egypt, and throughout Palestine, the teachers and their disciples pored over the Law and the prophets and prayed for God's rule of righteousness to be observed throughout the universe.

Then what had become of the hope of Israel? Israel's scriptural faith had been tried in this history, and differing understandings of the present and the future had become competitors. The realities of the Exile, the Hasmonean kingdom, the Judean kingship of Herod, and the Roman order had pitted various groups in Israel against one another. The stakes had become high with life, death, and the future of the people depending on differing convictions and practices. And in the era of Pontius Pilate, Jesus of Nazareth went from village to village in Galilee declaring the imminent appearance of the Kingdom of God.

Chapter 2

Jesus and the Prophets

The Facts of History and the Truth of the Gospels

Now Jesus did many other signs in the presence of the disciples, which are not written in this book; but these are written that you may believe that Jesus is the Christ, the Son of God, and that believing you may have life in his name. (Jn 20:30–1)
But there are also many other things which Jesus did; were every one of them to be written, I suppose that the world itself could not contain the books that would be written. (Jn 21:25)

The first book in this series is entitled *What Can We Know about Jesus?* What those who want to "understand Jesus today," want to know is often factual. What did Jesus actually say and do? Our sources do convey a great deal of such data, but they fail to relate many things we would like to know. The gospel writers were less interested in simply compiling the record, probably because they had heard so many things about Jesus, as the preceding quotes from John indicate (see also Lk 1:1–4).

That is not the only reason. What the gospel writers wanted the reader to know about Jesus was more theological than factual. That is, they wanted the reader to understand that Jesus is the agent and presence of God's will and reign in the world. This is at least a different kind of "fact." What can we know about Jesus? John's Gospel answers, "That he is the Messiah, the Son of God!" Of course such "knowledge" was not merely subjective opinion. It was a theological claim and conviction based on several kinds of "facts" from the Scriptures and experience. But it was not an indifferent "fact." It also meant faith in Jesus as God's way of ruling the world, now and in the future.

Modern readers often find the Gospels confusing because they are seeking the kinds of facts they could verify by scientific methods, that is, empirical facts. They begin to think that the gospel writers were too inventive or creative to be credible. They notice that the authors of the first three Gospels may tell the same story with significant variations in detail. The sequence of the episodes is also different in these "synoptic Gospels." So who has the good news straight? And then John's Gospel presents an elaborate dramatization of the Jesus story with long discourses. Readers begin to wonder if this is the same Jesus.

What they have noticed, of course, is that the Gospels were more dramatizations or depictions of Jesus than mere factual records. They were written probably about thirty-five to sixty years after the events they narrate, and they were primarily intended to tell the gospel truth about Jesus. They retold the traditional stories about what Jesus said and did in order to instruct and edify the readers. Their story included memories of what actually happened, but it also made constant selections and connections so that this story told the larger truth about God and Jesus. Thus the Gospels gathered up scriptural phrases and images tying this story to Israel's sacred heritage. They also reflected the way these stories had been told and retold in early Christian worship and recitations. This testimony is a richly woven tapestry of oriental stories where the details are full of meaning and faith.

It is foolish to criticize the Gospels for not providing more of the kind of information that a modern critical historian would accept as verifiable, and therefore true. What the gospel writers wanted their readers to know about Jesus will also prove instructive, and that will be the focus of Chapter 3.

On the other hand, it is still appropriate for modern readers to try to answer their questions about Jesus. The evangelists may have been primarily interested in attesting Jesus as God's prophet, Messiah, and judge of this world and the world to come, but what did Jesus himself teach about the future? To what extent did he interpret or predict the future in his words and deeds?

In order to answer such questions of historical fact it is necessary to examine the narratives by methods of comparison and contrast. This process poses questions that the Gospels were not primarily answering. For these purposes, the Gospels must be read not as testimonies of faith but as the only extensive records we possess of that past.

The limits of such methods must also be noted. All historical research can only produce probabilities. Even if sources are more specifically "factual," history is not a laboratory science where events may be repeated and "proved." And when historical events bear larger meanings, just knowing "the facts" is not adequate. The truth of history is a matter of both "what happened?" and "so what?"

Virtually the whole world has seen the film record of the assassination of President John Kennedy, and still the debate rages concerning both the fact and the meaning of "What really happened in Dallas?" Thus it is not surprising that the Gospels do not offer a direct photojournalistic depiction of Jesus or a merely objective account of his vision of the future. Jesus and his teaching were intensely significant for those who wrote the Gospels. Still, it is important and relatively possible to determine what Jesus of Nazareth said and did in the months and years leading up to the dramatic climax of his work in Jerusalem.

Jesus, the Galilean Prophet and Sage

In those days Jesus came from Nazareth of Galilee and was baptized by John in the Jordan. (Mk 1:9)

By all accounts, Jesus was a complex figure in his own time. The gospel writers probably enhance this element of mystery in order to require careful reading, but Jesus was also faced with various expectations. The question, "Who is this?", is still raised if any person begins to emerge with a public image or influence. In the ancient world, these questions of identity were tied even more directly into the sacred structures of time and space. Herod the Great might not have cared if Jesus was actually of Davidic descent. Still he might well have ordered all the boy babies in Bethlehem killed if he thought the people would believe that a son of David had been born "king of the Jews." The perception was as dangerous to Herod as the reality.

The Christian sources focus their presentations of Jesus on titles and identities that are filled with scriptural meanings. Jesus is confessed to be the Messiah or Christ, the Son of man, the Son of God, the Savior, and the Lord. It is possible that during the time of his own preaching, teaching, and healing, he was identified in such terms by his followers. Perhaps he even allowed some of these powerful scriptural identities to affect the way he pursued his work. But specific instances are very difficult to prove or disprove historically. The investments of later Christians in such titles and identities cast their shadow over earlier eras. It is likely that Jesus saw himself and was seen as enacting a mission of God, but which identities began with Jesus? Where did the interpretations of his followers or his adversaries enter the picture? How different was the story when it was told by Christian believers in later generations?

The facts that Jesus came from Galilee and was baptized in the Jordan River by John appear to be relatively secure. They even seem to be something of a problem for later presentations. Wasn't the Messiah supposed to come from Bethlehem in Judea? But Nazareth was in Galilee in the north. Luke 2 tells of Joseph and Mary traveling from Nazareth to Bethlehem on a special trip because of the census, and Matthew 2 relates how Jesus was taken to Nazareth for his own safety. In John 1:46 the question is even raised, "Can anything good come out of Nazareth?"

Similarly all the Gospels appear obliged to explain how it is that Jesus was baptized by John. Would not this make John superior to Jesus? Thus both Jesus' origin and his baptism gain in historical credibility because it is clear that they require interpretation in the tradition. What clues can they provide to identifying Jesus' own words or vision?

Much has been written about Jesus as a Galilean, often stressing that Galilee was a conquered territory of Judea. Parts of Galilee were very rural, and discontent ran high among the peasants, who bore an oppressive tax burden. Jesus' parables reflected agrarian culture. They were full of hope in the wonders God could do with seed, soil, and the birds of the air (see Mk 4:1–32; Mt 6:25–33). Some have suggested that Jesus was a rustic sage who called for God's restoration of land and flocks to disenfranchised peasants. The future he envisioned, therefore, was that of liberation of the poor from the yoke of Rome and their Judean vassals.

Others argue that Jesus was more a wandering charismatic teacher. His message was more spiritual, threatening only to those who were intent on defending the present order in God's name. His Galilee was a more cosmopolitan world than Judea in the south. His wisdom was that of an alternative view of reality, perhaps even influenced by the contemporary schools of the Cynics. A master of aphorisms, his sharply worded rejoinders to the orthodoxies of his time broke the molds of both religion and politics. The Kingdom of God he announced opened the future as an arena of gift and promise, unfettered by traditional rituals and justification.

Still others have focused on the intensity of John the Baptist's preaching of repentance. They have depicted Jesus as a self-styled inaugurator of the Reign of God announced by John. Like the sectarians at Qumran, John expected a cosmic revelation or apocalypse of God's Reign against the Gentiles and their sinful allies, especially in Jerusalem. Only the repentant could hope to "flee from the wrath to come" (Lk 3:7). Then Jesus, the Galilean prophet, claimed the freedom and authority of that kingdom, and he pressed toward the seat of power in Jerusalem in order to make the wheels of history turn.

This is the view Albert Schweitzer advanced in his famous book *The Quest of the Historical Jesus*. Schweitzer presented Jesus as determined, almost desperate to provoke God to act. Jesus believed that the time of judgment and of the final dawn of God's Kingdom had already begun, and he was committed to press that future forward himself. His dramatic entry into Jerusalem and cleansing of the Temple were prophetic acts. His death was an intended martyrdom, seeking to provoke God to initiate the future. Thus Jesus forced the Judean leadership to crush such dangerous presumption by handing him to Pilate.

All of these interpretations of Jesus and the future he announced accept the historical reliability of many aspects of the stories about Jesus: his Galilean origins, his baptism by John, his teaching in parables, his reputation as a healer and wonder worker, and his dramatic end in Jerusalem. Each of these interpretations also has some historical probability, but they cannot all be correct or even close to accurate at the same time. At points each may reveal more about the interpreters' convictions than about Jesus. That fact is a reminder that everything we know about Jesus is filtered through other people's views of him.

Yet even in their disagreements, these attempts to understand Jesus and his teaching about the future are instructive. They demonstrate that Jesus must be understood within his historical context, and they sharpen the questions of how Jesus' words and deeds related to his times. Thus the lengthy historical description given in Chapter 1 of this book is necessary. The question that must be answered first is where did Jesus fit in the range of views of Israel's hope for the future? And how did various people understand him?

Whether he was a prophet or a sage, Jesus was an interpreter of Israel's sacred tradition. He was compelled to enter the discussion of the fulfillment of God's promises. He must have had some education in scribal interpretation. Luke 4 refers to his reading the Scriptures, and John 6 reports that he wrote in the dust with his finger. He traveled from synagogue to synagogue in Galilee and taught everywhere he went. He may have regarded his teaching as a restatement of John's proclamation. Certainly his followers understood him this way. The critical question for all Israel was how God would fulfill the scriptural promises of salvation and restoration. Jesus took a distinctive position on this central hope.

The facts that he was from Galilee and was baptized by John do not provide evident answers to what Jesus was about. These facts only call for more precise interpretation, but they do set a focus for the questions. Jesus was one of several charismatic teachers who came from Galilee, and the tensions between the north and south were complex, economically as well as religiously. Jesus' teaching displayed a freedom or confidence that was a source of dismay to many teachers of Israel. Jesus announced and enacted a future that held peril for those who resisted God's Reign, but this Kingdom of God was full of promise for a new group of the "faithful." This Galilean prophet and sage stood out among the teachers of Israel's hope, but he can only be understood historically as one of them.

Jesus, Proclaimer of God's Gracious Reign

Now after John was arrested, Jesus came into Galilee, preaching the gospel of God, and saying, "The kingdom of God is at hand; repent, and believe in the gospel." (Mk 1:14–15)

The Christian Gospels present Jesus as a preacher of the gospel, but they remember that he proclaimed the coming of the Kingdom of God. Many other messages would be called "gospel" in Christian tradition, but according to Mark Jesus announced the nearness of God's Reign to be the "gospel of God." As Chapter 3 will show, Mark understood this to be a prediction. God is about to reveal a glorious reign of justice and mercy that has been hidden until now in suffering. Luke understood this to be a declaration. God has begun to reign in the ministry of Jesus, and the future will look like the dominion of this Lord and Messiah.

What was Jesus' vision of the present and future when he proclaimed God's Reign? Since this preaching of the "gospel of God" is so central to the Christian Gospels, they are more likely to give an interpretation of Jesus' preaching than a simple historical record. Is it possible to get behind their convictions to Jesus' own teaching?

The Friend of Tax Collectors and Sinners

One of the best routes to his teaching about God's Reign is through the gospel accounts of Jesus' disputes with adversaries. Of course the Gospels regard the things the adversaries say as misguided. The point of the Gospels is also not to provide extensive or fair-minded presentations of why Jesus' opponents said what they did. The first-century readers probably knew most of these views well. But these charges against Jesus give the modern reader access to a complex ancient discussion about God's Will and Reign. When they are taken seriously, they help identify what was offensive or new in Jesus' teaching.

In Matthew 11:18–19 and Luke 7:33–4, both evangelists quote a saying of Jesus that they have apparently taken from the "Sayings Source," called "Q." It is a fascinating report of the rejection of both John and Jesus on differing grounds: "John came neither eating nor drinking, and they say, 'He has a demon'; the Son of man came eating and drinking, and they say, 'Behold, a glutton and a drunkard, a friend of tax collectors and sinners.'" Such objections are obviously understood as wrongheaded, and they may originate from a later era of opposition to Jesus' disciples and John's. But they are summary judgments, certainly nothing the Christians would have created, and they fit with what the Gospels tell about John and Jesus.

John was an ascetic in the wilderness. His critics and friends agree that his diet was unusual (see Mt 3:4; Mk 1:6) and that his call for repentance was radical. The question was whether he was a prophet sent from God or a man possessed by demons, a lunatic. People who refused to listen to his announcement of impending judgment wrote him off. The scriptural promises and hopes of Israel could not be fulfilled this way. Of course the Gospels insist that many people in Israel from many groups went to hear John and to be baptized (Mt 3; Mk 1; Lk 3). For them he was the Elijah prophet of preparation (see Lk 1:16–17, 76; and Mal 3:1, 4:5). His adversaries rejected these marks of scriptural legitimacy as fraudulent or demonic.

The comparison with Jesus reveals a very different problem. As the Gospels indicate regularly, Jesus was no ascetic. He feasted often with his disciples and with persons whom the religiously careful disdained. This was particularly offensive in Israel, where food laws and rituals of eating were so much a part of the ceremonial law. These were matters not of mere hygiene but of purity before God. The separation of Israel from the Gentiles was marked by proper observance of the good laws. How else would Israel prove its faithfulness, its readiness for God's Reign?

Both Jesus and his disciples were accused of not washing properly before dinner (Lk 12:38; Mt 15:2; Mk 7:5), and the disciples were criticized for harvesting grain to eat on the Sabbath (Mk 2:23–4//Mt 12:1–2//Lk 6:1–2). Eating with tax collectors and sinners implied their acceptance by God. Some of these charges probably reflect a later era when Jesus' followers were in continuing conflict with the Pharisees, but the criticism goes back to Jesus.

Jesus' meal fellowship was a prophetic enactment. This was no longer the time of preparation, of ascetic denial that John had announced. The time of feasting had begun, and Jesus did not restrict his meal fellowship to those who were properly observant of the Law of Moses. Nor did he accept their view of the scrupulous observance of the Sabbath. The Gospels concur that he did dine with those whom the scribes and Pharisees regarded as "sinners," and he did not insist that the tax collector (see Lk 19:1–10) or the sinner repent first (see Lk 7:36–50). The objection of his adversaries is even the occasion for the Gospels to stress Jesus' distinctive mission of the kingdom: "Those who are well have no need of a physician, but those who are sick; I have not come to call the righteous, but sinners" (Mk 2:15–17).

Luke's version (5:32) of this word of Jesus has softened the offense by emphasizing that Jesus intended to call these sinners "to repentance." Of course the Pharisees were also intent on calling sinners to repentance. Yet even in Luke, the Pharisees were shocked when Jesus ate with sinners and tax collectors before they were properly repentant or observant of the Law. The Pharisees and John believed that God would yet deliver on the promises and the warnings to Israel. Proper observance of the Law by all of Israel and even severe acts of repentance were in order to prepare for that future. But Jesus acted as if the feasting of the Kingdom had already begun, and the strangest assortment of people were invited to the festivities.

Jesus' friendship with tax collectors and sinners was not merely sentimental. It was a decisive act, a vision of God's program for the future of Israel. It fit with his words of blessing on the poor, the hungry, the grieving, and the outcasts (see Lk 6 and Mt 5). These were declarations of the priorities of God's Reign. It may not be possible to establish historically that Jesus was called Messiah or Lord or even Son of man in his lifetime. But his strategy of reaching out to those on or beyond the fringe of acceptability was clear to adversaries and disciples. It altered the logic and pressed the question of his authority.

The larger historical arena must be recalled again. Jesus the Galilean was not in the same orbit as the Herodians or high priests or Sadducees who were striving to preserve the Temple and the sanctity of Israel within the Roman system. He was rather participating in a scribal debate, a complex of alternative understandings of the way that God's promises and judgment would be fulfilled. His vision of God's unconditional acceptance of tax collectors and sinners set him apart from the preachers of repentance. He did not reject the Law and the prophets, but he refused to see the law as the basis or condition for the restoration of God's Rule. He dared to offer a distinctive prophetic interpretation of the scriptural promises. He declared God's will and reign to be gracious and accepting of those whom the religious leaders identified as sinners. He even agreed that he, like God, was the friend of sinners. Such a method could be dangerous if it generated a popular movement. It was certainly a heresy from the point of those who saw the fulfillment of the Law of Moses as God's assurance of Israel's future security.

The Prayer for the Kingdom

The Gospels are like mosaic depictions of Jesus' life and mission. The final composition is the statement of the evangelist, but the pieces within the composition may be very old. Certain words and prayers of Jesus have been preserved and transmitted exactly this way. These were generally memory pieces, bits of the oral tradition that were treasured and repeated in Christian worship and stories. These sayings were translated into Greek at a very early stage, and scholars debate whether they may be able to reconstruct the exact words Jesus used in his Semitic dialect called Aramaic.

The prayer that Jesus taught his disciples is generally called "The Lord's Prayer," but might well be called the prayer for the Kingdom. Like many other Jewish prayers of the era, it invokes God's Reign. Even in modern usage, there is nothing specifically Christian about its contents, and it is never prayed in Jesus' name. The most ancient form of the prayer is probably found in Luke 11:2b–4. It is strikingly brief. It does not make an elaborate theological statement as if to instruct God. But its whole thrust is to petition God's future reign into the present. It expresses Jesus' conviction about God and the future.

The prayer is decisively about this world. Matthew's version, which speaks about God "in heaven," is even more emphatic that the prayer is for God's will and reign "on earth as in heaven" (Mt 6:9–13). Neither Jesus nor his followers needed to pray for God's will or reign to come in heaven. It was already there. But earth needed the prayer because it needed the Kingdom. The petitions for daily bread, forgiveness as we have forgiven, and freedom from temptation all indicate the substance of God's Rule in contrast to the present order. These are human concerns, and they express Jesus' confidence in God's gracious will. Neither God nor God's Kingdom is a threat or peril for those who pray. Forgiveness is a way of life because it is the way of God's Kingdom.

Perhaps Jesus' prayer had an even stronger future orientation than is evident in English. Some interpreters argue that this was a prayer that the bread of the kingdom to come be given to the faithful in the present. Perhaps the temptation to be avoided is also a future test or crisis. Certainly the prayer expresses a sharp awareness that God's Reign is far from evident in the present. But this is not a prayer for the end of the world. Jesus was calling on God to exercise dominion among the faithful in this world.

Parables of the Kingdom

The parables of Jesus are also glimpses of Jesus' teaching about the present and future kingdom. Many of them are especially surprising when lifted out of the literary contexts of the Gospels. Extensive study of the parables has confirmed that many of them could be traced through the oral tradition back to Jesus. Some of them were simple allegories or object lessons, but others were quite unusual in their form and message. Jesus' distinctive mark remains on several of the parables of the Kingdom.

In his telling, these parables were filled with the same confidence and liberty as were his meals with tax collectors and sinners. They also had the hope for the future of his Kingdom prayer. The steward of unrighteousness (Lk 16:1–9) and the unrighteous judge (Lk 18:1–8) could never be remodeled into examples of virtue. The farmer who scatters seed on the ground and then goes home to bed (Mk 4:26–9) would not be praised for his diligence. The element of the unexpected proves to be an occasion for a revelation about the extravagance of God's grace, God's concern for those who cry to him, or the assurance of the ultimate triumph of God's Reign. Many people told stories to illustrate morality lessons, but these parables of Jesus disclosed the grandeur and power of God's mercy.

When the early Christians and the evangelists began explaining these parables, they also were tempted to turn them into morality lessons. Jesus' Parable of the Incredible Harvest of the Kingdom against All Odds (Mk 4:3–9//Mt 13:3–9//Lk 8:5–8) became an allegory on various responses to preaching. The shocking freedom of Jesus' words about God was transformed into a lesson. But the parable itself survived in the image of the multifold harvest in the face of great obstacles. At its heart, the parable testified to Jesus' boundless confidence in God's mercy with very little interest in morality lessons. The Kingdom of God is not a program to be ushered in with careful observance of the rules, even observance of the Law of Moses. The Kingdom of God is a gift, not a reward for observance. As Luke (12:32) quotes Jesus, "Fear not little flock, for it is your Father's good pleasure to give you the kingdom."

These were shocking words. The Gospels knew that the offense of the parables was closely connected with Jesus' acceptance of tax collectors and sinners. Matthew grouped many of his parables in Chapter 13 and concluded the section with the offense that was taken at Jesus. Their question was, "Where did this man get this wisdom and these mighty works?", and its meaning was that no one has authority for such talk!

In Luke 15, the classic parables of the Lost Sheep, Lost Coin, and Loving Father were offered as responses to the criticism that Jesus "receives sinners and eats with them." Jesus' emphasis on God's preoccupation with the lost was offensive to the religiously upright. What would happen to the urgency of their efforts to restore all of Israel to observing the Law?

It has been said that no one would bother to execute a wandering teacher who told parables. This might have been true for Jesus if Israel's internal conflicts had not been so deep or the stakes so high. The future was in peril.

This was a traditional oriental culture where the authority of those who interpret the faith was a matter of great social consequence. Sanctions against heresy are still matters of life and death in some Arab or African cultures, and popular teachers may gather large followings. Obscure religious leaders may become the center of attention and controversy when the structures of authority are under attack.

Jesus' parables could not be taken lightly. They were revelations of an astonishing grace in God's Reign, and they were heard as threats by those who held other views of how God reigns. But for those who could only trust God to receive the Kingdom and the future as a gift, the parables were assurances of hope.

Healings and Exorcisms: Signs of the World to Come

Jesus was known as a healer, an exorcist, and a worker of wonders. It is not possible to prove scientifically that he performed impossible "miracles." The whole point even in the ancient world was that such acts were incredible and impossible for human beings. But healers and exorcists were more common in that culture, and the fact that Jesus had such a reputation was not so remarkable. The Pharisees and Essenes counted some famous healers among their numbers. The controversy surrounding his reputation was much more significant. His healings, exorcisms, and mighty acts made statements about him and about God. His disciples and adversaries agreed that they were claims about the way God's Reign was breaking into the present. No one could take these acts lightly.

His reputation as a healer was linked for his adversaries with his healing on the Sabbath. Numerous stories in the Gospels relate the disputes and antagonism he provoked by Sabbath healings. Healers were always to be watched since they were thought to possess powers or might be frauds. But healing on the Sabbath appeared to some to be testing God. "There are six days on which work ought to be done," said a ruler of the synagogue to the people in Luke 13. "Come on those days and be healed, and not on the Sabbath."

In Mark 3:4 Jesus confronts such views directly with a word that summarizes the conflict: "Is it lawful on the Sabbath to do good or to do harm, to save a life or to kill?" This may not be a verbatim quotation from the historical Jesus, but it reflects the kind of controversy over the will of God that Jesus' healings produced. Jesus reportedly entered directly into this discussion of the proper interpretation of the Scriptures (see Lk 13:15; Mt 12:11). These were not foolish questions for those in Israel who were intent on being faithful to the Law, but the Gospels never suggest that Jesus accepted restrictions on Sabbath healing.

Jesus' exorcisms of evil spirits were even more sharply divisive. His strong assertion of authority to heal on the Sabbath probably contributed to this division. What kind of power did Jesus represent? Was it conceivable that someone who overrode the sanctity of the Sabbath could be endowed with power and authority from God? Or was this already a clue that Jesus' power was demonic? This is exactly the accusation to which Jesus responds in the synoptic gospel accounts (Mt 12:24–30, 9:34; Mk 3:22–7; Lk 11:15–27; see also Jn 7:20; 8:48, 52; 10:20): "He is possessed by Beelzebul, and by the prince of demons he casts out the demons!" (Mk 3:22).

The Christian authors would certainly not have introduced this charge if it had not first been raised by others against Jesus. The issue relates directly to the question of the future because Jesus is either bringing the Kingdom of God with its promise or he is an agent of the powers of deceit and destruction. The Gospels agree that Jesus' answer met the objection directly. "How can Satan cast out Satan? If a kingdom is divided against itself, that house will not be able to stand" (Mk 3:23–4). Luke's (11:20) and Matthew's (12:28) versions press the matter further, drawing on a traditional saying from Q: "But if it is by the finger (Matt. Spirit of God) of God that I cast out demons, then the kingdom of God has come upon you."

The Christian Gospels elaborated these claims. They were sure that Jesus' healings, exorcisms, and mighty acts were signs of the fulfillment of God's promises. In Mark 2:1–12, the healing of the paralytic demonstrated that Jesus had the authority "on earth to forgive sins." This was the authority of the heavenly Son of man of Daniel's (7:13) prophecy. In Matthew 14:22–33, Jesus' stilling of the storm displayed the power that only God had in the Psalms and prophets to overcome the forces of the deep. In Luke 7:11–17 when Jesus raised the widow's son from the dead, he was revealed as a "great prophet" like Elijah and a visitation of God. The evangelists confidently portrayed these acts as signs of the incursion of God's Reign. Jesus was opening the future of health, safety, and freedom promised by God.

It may not be possible to know exactly how Jesus understood his wonders. But the conflict they generated was much like that produced by his friendship with tax collectors and sinners, his disputes about the Sabbath, his prayers and his parables. His mighty deeds sharpened the question of his authority as proclaimer of God's gracious reign. His priority for the disabled and possessed again drove to the question of how God's Rule works. His could not be a conditional system with the Law as a binding standard. Jesus was acting with a kind of messianic license. He was exercising an authority in which his acts of mercy were above the law, even the Law of God. Yet he was proclaiming the Kingdom of God. He was inaugurating a distinctive program of God's reign. He and his adversaries could agree. This was either a demonic perversion of God's will or its decisive enactment.

Jesus, Predictor of a Dire Future

And when he drew near and saw the city he wept over it, saying, "Would that even today you knew the things that make for peace! But now they are hid from your eyes. For the days shall come upon you, when your enemies will cast up a bank about you and surround you, and hem you in on every side, and dash you to the ground, you and your children within you, and they will not leave one stone upon another in you; because you did not know the time of your visitation. (Lk 19:41–4)

It is difficult to achieve an objective picture of the historical Jesus. Several factors complicate the effort. The first is that the gospel sources are primarily interested in proclaiming him to be the resurrected Lord of heaven and earth. The memories of what he said and did are enhanced and ordered to convey the Christian faith in him as God's agent and ruler. As suggested earlier, it is foolish to complain that the Gospels are testimonies of faith, but it limits their immediate usefulness for historical research on Jesus.

A second factor is that Jesus was himself a controversial figure, and he was enmeshed in the complex debates in Israel about how God's Rule works in the world. His disciples and Christian interpreters were also not of one mind on these matters, and they perceived him in a variety of ways. What did he say about the Kingdom of God and what did he mean? Not only were his adversaries confused and angry, his followers also heard what he said differently. They came with differing convictions about God. They had a variety of social origins, and they lived their lives in differing times and situations.

Had human history become so perverted that God could only save the world by purging it with fire? Was there any hope that Israel could be led to repentance and trust in the kingdom that Jesus proclaimed? Did Jesus believe that God was about to restore a future of promise to the faithful?

The historical complexities do not obscure Jesus' confidence in God's gracious reign. At every turn in the traditions about him, his assurance of the depth of God's mercy and justice emerges. His conviction of the ultimate triumph of the righteous rule of the God of Israel was firm. When he proclaimed the nearness of the Kingdom of God, he was probably not predicting the end of this world, but he was declaring that God's promises to Israel were coming to fulfillment. One scholar of Jesus' teaching on the Kingdom, Bruce Chilton, proposes that Jesus was saying, "God is gathering strength!" This was the basis of his own authority to take liberties with the Law and to reach out to the marginalized. It was also the source of his offense to many in Israel. He appeared to take God's Law in his own hands.

It is important to note that Jesus was in good scriptural company. The prophets of Israel had long testified to God's dynamic rule in justice and in mercy. The specific word of the Lord to Israel would vary according to the realities of the times. There was a time to speak oracles of doom and a time to pronounce restoration. The prophets were not particularly original. In fact, consistency with the heritage of prophetic declarations was much more important. They used and restated old oracles repeatedly. Yet their declarations could strike home with particular force when their word from God was a timely address.

Jeremiah denounced the false prophets for speaking "Peace, peace, when there is not peace!" (Jer 6:14; 8:11; Ez 13:10). In different times, Isaiah 40:1–2 would declare God's consolation and restoration of Israel: "Speak tenderly to Jerusalem and cry to her that her warfare is ended, that her iniquity is pardoned." And both prophetic declarations were secure in the conviction that God is the ruler of history.

Jesus' announcement of God's gracious reign was therefore a prophetic word. His authority to speak and act with such dramatic freedom was a source of controversy. Was he truly God's prophet or perhaps even the anointed one or Messiah who would bring in God's Reign? His warnings of judgment were directed toward those who rejected him and his program of the Kingdom. Jesus confronted Israel with a particular definition of God's Rule.

The historical environment again illumines the reality of his mission. While Jesus was still in Galilee, Herod Antipas, grandson of Herod the Great, had already executed John the Baptist (Mt 14:1–12; Mk 6:17–18; Lk 3:19–20; Josephus, *Antiquities* 18.116–19). Prophetic preachers of repentance often found themselves in peril with rules. The Gospels report indirect threats to Jesus from Herod, who may have associated him with John (Mt 14:1–2; Mk 6:14–16; Lk 9:7–9; 13:31–5). The Gospels and Josephus also indicate that Pontius Pilate was proving to be disrespectful or hostile toward Jewish religious traditions. Luke 13:1 alludes to "the Galileans whose blood Pilate had mingled with their sacrifices," and Josephus tells of Pilate provoking riots in Jerusalem by bringing in a statue of the emperor and by using money from the Temple treasury to build an aqueduct (*Antiquities* 18.55–62).

Some of these events may have occurred later, but Jesus' prophetic mission of the Kingdom was conducted in the midst of growing tensions in Galilee and Judea. His conviction of God's gracious strength posed a challenge. This was not a strategy of ascetic withdrawal awaiting God's intervention in judgment against the sinners. It was not a retreat into meticulous observance of the Law, gathering all of the righteous into a band of the elect. It was also not a cautious policy of preserving the Temple and its sacrifices at all costs. It was a prophetic declaration that God was now initiating God's Reign.

The restoration of the sinners, the poor, and the disabled had already begun, in accord with the ancient prophetic promises of restoration. The salvation and future of Israel lay with those who could see and hear and trust the reality of God's Reign.

Jesus was confident of this declaration, but he was not naive. This is a difficult but important issue. It is difficult because the Gospels have enlarged on Jesus' warnings to his followers about the perils that lay ahead. By the time the Gospels were written, Jesus' disciples had endured considerable suffering and exclusion. Jesus' words of warning were rehearsed to assure the Christians that such problems had been anticipated.

But even earlier, Jesus' prophetic confidence in God was never naive optimism. None of the Gospels gives any hint that Jesus promised quick success or easy rewards. On the contrary, his same prophetic confidence in God's ultimate reign necessitated his denunciation of false comforts and faithless ways to peace. His program of the Kingdom was a declaration of God's way of peace and salvation for Israel. It was also a prophetic warning against impending doom.

The Gospels insist that Jesus was pessimistic about the days that would soon come for Israel. His prophetic declaration of God's gracious rule also envisioned an almost inevitable catastrophe for those who resisted this reign. As in Israel's more apocalyptic prophetic traditions, Jesus probably saw the forces of evil set on an irreversible course of conflict with the Reign of God. Then the events of history were directly caught up in a cosmic struggle of forces and powers in heaven and earth.

In Mark 13, Jesus is depicted largely as such a prophet, predicting a dire future with help from the prophecies of Daniel (see Chapter 3). Jesus probably contributed to Israel's many interpretations of the book of Daniel, but his prophecy was not so speculative. Mark 13:32 emphasized that Jesus did not know the whole future in advance: "But of that day or that hour no one knows, not even the angels in heaven, nor the Son, but only the Father." Whatever Jesus may have said about the future on the basis of Daniel, he did not lay out a cryptic blueprint in advance.

He probably did warn of a coming calamity in Israel. Perhaps he even foresaw the possible captivity and destruction of Jerusalem and the Temple. But this was prophetic insight, tied directly to the rejection he was experiencing in his program of the Kingdom. Either he was the agent of God's Kingdom or not. And if so, his proclamation was the key to Israel's salvation or doom.

The prophetic warnings and oracles of the Scriptures were regularly conditional. Jeremiah's (22:5) oracle against the Temple is a famous example: "If you will not heed these words, I swear by myself, says the Lord that his house shall become a desolation." Jesus' oracles had the same logic, "Unless you repent you will all likewise perish!" (Lk 13:3, 5). In this case, repentance meant not simply remorse for sin. Jesus' whole ministry was a call to conversion to his distinctive vision of how God rules the world.

It is also possible, but less sure, that he concluded that most of Israel and its leadership would not accept him or the Reign of God he announced. Then he may have been caught up in a prophet's pathos over the dire fate ahead. Luke's (13:31–5; 19:41–4; 21:20–4) accounts of Jesus' tears for Jerusalem could go back to Jesus, although their present form fits the context of the gospel well. These oracles are heavily weighted with the phrases of the dire words Jeremiah spoke before the first destruction of Jerusalem. Later in the first century another prophet, also named Jesus, reportedly paraphrased Jeremiah 7:34 in an oracle of doom: "A voice from the east, a voice from the west, a voice from the four winds; a voice against Jerusalem and the sanctuary, a voice against the bridegroom and the bride, a voice against all the people!" (Josephus, *War* 6.301). It is historically credible that Jesus of Nazareth announced judgment on a Jerusalem that did not accept the gracious Kingdom of God he announced.

Jesus, Determined to Trust God

At that very hour some Pharisees came, and said to him, "Get away from here, for Herod wants to kill you." And he said to them, "Go and tell that fox, 'Behold, I cast out demons and perform cures today and tomorrow, and the third day I finish my course. Nevertheless I must go on my way today and tomorrow and the day following; for it cannot be that a prophet should perish away from Jerusalem.'" (Lk 13:31–3)

What about Jesus' future? Did he predict his own death? This is a very difficult historical question, and many people think it has serious consequences for Jesus' credibility and legitimacy.

All of the Gospels answer with a clear conviction that Jesus anticipated his own end. They insist that he was neither naive nor suicidal, but he went to Jerusalem knowing that his life was at stake. But the Gospels vary in their estimations of how much Jesus knew of what would happen to him.

The possibility of ignorance of the political dangers deserves attention. Several of the rustic prophets and deluded heroes in Josephus' stories probably underestimated the hazards of missions to Jerusalem. Luke 9:51–3 tells of the Samaritans' aversion to Jesus when he set his face to go to Jerusalem. That episode could mean several things, but the fear of associating with anyone with such dangerous intentions is plausible. Such stories also suggest that Jesus would have had ample warnings from friends and adversaries. Simple ignorance is not credible.

Albert Schweitzer regarded Jesus' several predictions in Mark (8:31; 9:31; 10:33–4) of his death by crucifixion as based on memories of Jesus' own words. He emphasized that Jesus' triumphal entry as a royal figure (Mk 11:1–10) and purging the Temple of money changers (Mk 11:15–17) were prophetic enactments. Jesus was playing out the role of the heavenly Son of man. He was seeking to throw himself on the wheel of apocalyptic history, to put the final events in motion and to prompt God to act. He was on a kind of martyr's mission to bring in the Kingdom. Jesus' last words in Mark (15:34) are thus also a historical memory of a disappointed prophet, "My God, my God, why has thou forsaken me?"

The irony is that Schweitzer, thinking that Mark was simplistic, probably picked up Mark's view of prophecy and history. As the next chapter will show, Mark stresses the apocalyptic character of Jesus' words and death, but Mark certainly did not regard Jesus as deluded. Schweitzer grasped the cosmic confrontation that Mark was depicting in Jesus' death, but he missed the evangelist's conviction that this apparent defeat was God's triumph.

Still Jesus' dramatic entry into Jerusalem and his symbolic cleansing of the Temple were the right historical clues. Only someone who had a sense of being on a mission from God would come unarmed into Jerusalem like a king. And only someone with a fearless confidence would risk an interference in the Temple and its financial arena. If Jesus was determined to carry out these actions as he approached Jerusalem, his predictions of death by crucifixion would have been sensible. They would not even have required divine inspiration. That is an important historical judgment, and it goes as far as historical research can proceed. Critical historiography cannot directly confirm or disprove whether Jesus was being led by God or even if he knew it.

On the other hand, these symbolic prophetic actions of Jesus' entry and cleansing fit with Jesus' proclamation of the Kingdom of God. Jerusalem and the Temple were not merely places, but focal symbols of the identity of Israel. This king who "comes in the name of the Lord" (Mk 11:9; Mt 21:1–9; Lk 19:28–38) into Jerusalem was fulfilling scriptural precedents (see Ps 118:26; Zec 9:9). Such actions were fully consistent for a proclaimer of the Kingdom of God. Even the reports that Jesus was apparently unarmed and hailed by a broad populace fit with the kind of reign his parables, healings, and meal fellowships had exhibited.

Those previous declarations of how God has chosen to reign had evoked conflict from the leadership in the synagogues and the ascetics in the wilderness. This was not the way of God or the way into future safety according to their convictions. Their opposition of Jesus had grown in intensity as rejection of false teaching.

Now the conflict would be a matter of life and death, and the response would be quick. Jesus had entered the volatile climate of occupied Jerusalem in the midst of the religious festival of Passover. His humble procession might be no direct threat to the troops in the Roman garrison or the Temple guards, but he was sending a message. Other groups in Palestine might well cheer to see him disrupt the financial enterprise of the Temple. Those who denounced the "wicked priest" from the safety of the wilderness might be especially gratified. The mixture of admiration and disdain that some held for Herod's beautiful temple would certainly produce confusion in others if Jesus actually predicted its destruction (see Mk 13:1–2; Mt 24:1–3; Lk 21:5–7). But Jesus was continuing on his determined mission to announce and enact a distinctive vision of the Reign of God.

As noted earlier, the Romans valued the Roman peace as a sacred trust. That was why Pilate was in town, and probably why Herod Antipas came down from Galilee at the time of the Passover. For them, peace and security and the future lay with preventing insurrection. Their Judean appointees in the high priesthood were also compelled to keep the peace, at any cost. The high priests also understood the continuity of the Temple sacrifices to be their sacred trust in the midst of the Roman system. That was the key to Israel's peace and security. That was how the Reign of God in Israel was sustained under the Roman order.

The execution of Jesus, therefore, was fully predictable. Perhaps one would say that it was historically inevitable since the conflict drove to the heart of how God reigns. What kind of kingdom is legitimate for God and humanity? In what dominion do future peace and security lie?

Chapter 3

Jesus and the Kingdom

The Vindication of Jesus

And being found in human form, he humbled himself and became
obedient until death, even death on a cross. Therefore God has highly
exalted him and bestowed on him the name which is above every
name; that at the name of Jesus every knee should bow, in heaven and
on earth and under the earth, and every tongue confess that Jesus
Christ is the Lord to the glory of God the Father. (Phil 2:8–11)
Let all the house of Israel therefore know assuredly that God has made
him both Lord and Christ, this Jesus whom you crucified. (Acts 2:36)

Many prophets have made predictions about the future, and in
some traditions the prophet is a mere technician reading the
cosmic signs. But the prophets of Israel understood their words
of warning and promise to be revelations of God's Reign and
plan of action. They did not predict a coldly fated future, but
one that was as sure as God's compassionate will. The exact
future could even change while God's unswerving purpose remained constant. If the people would repent, God could alter
the future.

These prophets were agents, declaring security and destruction, initiating God's dominion by their very words. The response of the people to the prophets' declarations was, therefore, crucial to their future. Present historical realities were
critical occasions where the future hung in the balance, and
even the prophetic predictions were tests of the people's obedience. Those who rejected or killed the prophets were contending with God, putting God's word and reign to the test.

And what would happen if the rulers and people killed the

one who declared and even inaugurated God's Reign? What would be their future? What would God do about a truly righteous prophet? "Let us see if his words are true," say the scoffers in the Wisdom of Solomon, "and let us test what will happen at the end of his life; for if the righteous man is God's son, he will help him, and will deliver him from the hand of his adversaries" (Wisd 2:17–18).

The entire New Testament is written in the confidence that Jesus was wrongfully killed and that God raised the crucified Messiah from the dead and exalted him as Lord of heaven and earth. The Resurrection is not understood merely as a proof of life after death for humanity. It is a vindication of Jesus. It is a revelation of the "secret wisdom" of the Kingdom of God that "the rulers of this age" did not understand when they crucified Jesus (1 Cor 2:7–8). The Resurrection is God's ultimate endorsement of Jesus' words, deeds, faithfulness, and rule. The faith that God raised the crucified Jesus is crucial to everything the New Testament says about Jesus and the future.

Even before the books of the New Testament were written, followers of this resurrected Messiah were proclaiming, "Jesus is Lord." They believed the accounts of his disciples who were "witnesses to the Resurrection," and they understood his altered physical presence to be a sign of a glorious new state of being (see Lk 24; Jn 20; 1 Cor 15:35–50). This was the work of God, confirming Jesus as God's Messiah and then exalting him to heavenly dominion far above the kings and emperors before whose names the world bowed in fear.

But what then did Jesus mean for the future? Was not resurrection merely a peril for humanity? Would not his reappearance or return portend destruction? How could the early Christians understand his exaltation as "good news"?

The exact wording and form of earliest Christian preaching are no longer known. It can only be estimated from reading Paul's letters, which were written about twenty years after the time of Jesus (50s) or from the Gospels and Acts, which were probably written another fifteen to thirty years later (70s to 80s).

These documents contain memory pieces, hymns, confessions, and dramatized depictions of the preaching of the apostles. They demonstrate the vitality and intense expectation of the faith of earliest Christianity. They also indicate that for those early followers, Jesus was the fundamental revelation of the future of the world, of Israel and the nations, and of their own future. That future did include peril and judgment for those who continued to resist God's Reign, but it was full of hope for those who trusted and obeyed the reign of the exalted Lord.

The historical memory of Jesus' execution as "King of the Jews" was foundational for their vision of the future. In the Resurrection, God confirmed Jesus as the "anointed one," which is the exact translation of the Hebrew title "Messiah" or the Greek title "Christ." Whether or not this title had been used directly for Jesus in his lifetime, it interpreted the ironic truth of the title above his head on the cross.

As Chapters 1 and 2 have shown, various Jewish groups had held differing views of Israel's common hope in God's Rule. Now the followers of the Messiah Jesus proclaimed the surprising fulfillment of this hope. Jesus was indeed the "King of the Jews," but not because Pilate sarcastically said so. God declared him to be the royal Messiah or Christ because of his obedience to the death to God's will and reign.

The verses from Philippians 2 and Acts 2 cited at the beginning of this chapter are such Christian testimonies. They are traditional affirmations that were preserved in the context of these New Testament books, and they declare Jesus' divine authority and dominion. Jesus still had everything to do with the future, but not simply as one who formerly made predictions. This crucified Messiah had now been raised by God and exalted to rule. The "Messianists" or "Christians" announced a distinctive fulfillment of God's promises to Israel. Those who sought to secure their future or defend the Temple by eliminating Jesus had made a devastating mistake. The future belonged to the Messiah, not to the Temple, the Torah, or even to Caesar.

The title "Christ" or "Messiah" was a traditional Jewish designation. In the New Testament, it refers almost exclusively to Jesus' divinely authorized role as king or ruler. This title is so emphatically linked with Jesus' execution that Paul summarized his own message by saying, ". . . we preached Christ crucified, a stumbling block to Jews and a folly to Gentiles, but to those who are called, both Jews and Greeks, Christ the power of God and the wisdom of God" (1 Cor 1:23–4).

The title "Lord" was used much more broadly in the Roman world to speak of Caesar's divinely authorized dominion. This usage itself had a long previous history. For centuries, oriental rulers had claimed the title "Lord," and the scriptures of Israel had confronted these claims with mighty declarations that only God is Lord: "I am the LORD, that is my name; my glory I give to no other" (Is 42:8).

For some Jews of the first century this conviction was even a basis for revolt against the Roman overlords since God alone was to be revered as Lord. Josephus reported that some endured torture and death in their refusal to declare the fundamental pledge of Roman allegiance, "Caesar is lord" (*War* 7.411, 418–19).

The Christian confession "Jesus is Lord" was, therefore, full of meaning. But how could it be true? The dominion of Jesus over heaven and earth was far from evident. Furthermore, most of the leaders in Israel regarded Jesus as a false prophet. Many of these officials were probably very unhappy that Jesus or any other Jew had been executed by Roman crucifixion. No community chooses to turn to the occupation army to settle its religious disputes. But once such an execution had happened, the declaration that Jesus was raised, vindicated, and exalted by God to rule was even more unacceptable (see Acts 3–5).

When the early Christians declared, "Jesus is Lord!" or "God has made him Lord and Messiah, this Jesus whom you crucified!", they were announcing that Jesus was the key to the future that God was determined to accomplish. This future was unacceptable and dangerous to the future that the Roman order and their Judean rulers had in mind.

It is important to note that we are now discussing what Jesus meant to his Christian followers. In the preceding chapter, we were considering what Jesus himself intended by his words and acts during his historical lifetime. Scholars often distinguish between the Christ of faith and the historical Jesus. Many historians are only mildly interested in the Christian faith in Jesus as the Christ. They would agree that the New Testament is full of such faith, but they are only concerned with what Jesus himself thought about the future. They are also quick to point out that Jesus' followers did not all have the same understanding of what his significance was for the future.

On the other hand, the early Christians were not interested in mere historical reconstruction. The times were changing, and their declarations of hope in Jesus constantly confronted new challenges. Their memories of what Jesus himself said and did were infused with the faith that God had raised him from the dead. Jesus was not a mere predictor whose accuracy could now be checked. His words and deeds were remembered and recited in the light of Easter. The future lay in the hands of this Jesus whom God had raised from the dead.

Our historical study of Jesus and the future is as interested in this Christ of faith as it was in the historical Jesus. This proves to be the next chapter in the history that began with Abraham, David, and the return from Babylon. Israel's hopes in the promises of God were the threads that held together the tattered skein of Judean history through the Greek, Hasmonean, and early Roman centuries. But these hopes were far from uniform, as we have seen.

Jesus' distinctive vision of how God's dominion would be restored was a challenge to official systems and theologies, and he was put to death. Now his followers would continue to confront changing times with their conviction that Jesus is God's vindicated Lord and Messiah. They preserved and translated the sayings and stories of Jesus, confident that this Christ of faith is Lord of history and of the future.

In the ensuing decades, the apostles and evangelists told and retold the story of Jesus in order to bear witness to his faith. Christian hope in Jesus as Lord and Messiah of God's future was constant. That hope and story of Jesus, however, assumed differing forms, tones, and details as historical realities changed.

Paul, a Servant of Jesus Christ

For all things are yours, whether Paul or Apollos or Cephas or the world or life or death or the present or the future, all are yours; and you are Christ's and Christ is God's. (1 Cor 3:21–3)

About twenty years after Jesus' crucifixion, Paul of Tarsus was traveling through Asia Minor, Greece, Palestine, and Rome as an "apostle" and "servant" of Jesus Christ. His letters that survive in the New Testament tell no stories of Jesus, and they hardly mention the Kingdom of God. Nevertheless, Paul's entire mission among Jews and Gentiles was filled with the confidence in the Messiah Jesus' gift of salvation, vindication, the present, and the future.

Those years were difficult for Israel. The quality of Roman rule in Palestine continued to decline. The governors who succeeded Pontius Pilate reflected a growing leadership crisis in Rome and a decreasing patience with Jewish particularity. First-century Jewish authors regularly lamented the plight of the Jews in a system that was increasingly despotic.

The emperor Gaius Caligula (37–41) went out of his way to scapegoat the Jews. He played local leaders in Alexandria against the Jewish community and taunted the Jewish embassy that came to Rome seeking a hearing. He appointed Herod Agrippa I, the grandson of Herod the Great, as "king of the Jews," although Agrippa had only minimal acquaintance with Palestine.

Caligula's conflict with the Jews was at once political and theological because he insisted that he be worshiped as the divine emperor. He ordered his effigy set up for worship in the Temple in Jerusalem, provoking mass protests in the streets. Even Herod Agrippa pleaded with Caligula to back down, and the governor in Syria saw that the emperor's adamance would produce open rebellion. The governor put his own life at risk by disobeying Caligula's order, and he was spared only by the timely assassination of the emperor.

The next emperor, Claudius (41–54), was less hostile to the Jews and not eager to be acclaimed divine. But he dealt sternly with the Jews in Egypt and appointed inept and abusive governors in Palestine. He also expelled the Jews from the city of Rome, including Paul's associates, Priscilla and Aquila (Acts 18:1–4). He appointed Herod Agrippa II to succeed Agrippa I at his death, and this king was merely a Roman vassal throughout all of the agonizing years of the Jewish rebellion.

Paul's life probably ended with his execution in the era of Nero (54–68). That emperor blamed the Jews and "the followers of a certain Chrestus" for his burning of Rome. Throughout the reigns of Claudius and Nero, Paul experienced frequent imprisonments and conflicts with the Roman and Jewish authorities. It is hard to see how any Jew, including Paul, could continue to believe that God's promised reign and righteousness held any promise for Israel or the world. Paul's letters emphasized that his proclamation of Jesus appeared to be a stumbling block to the Jews and a folly to the Greeks.

Nevertheless, Paul's confidence in the future was remarkable. He continued to announce that the heavenly reign of the Lord Jesus would soon be revealed over all principalities and powers. "Salvation is nearer to us now than when we first believed," he said (Rom 13:11).

The earliest book in the New Testament is probably Paul's first letter "to the church of the Thessalonians" (1 Thes 1:1). This letter is filled with the counsel of the apostle who encourages and charges the community "like a father with his children" (2:11). Their relationship with him is linked with their relationship with the Lord Jesus. Paul is their instructor, "gentle as a nurse" in his care for them: "So being affectionately desirous of you, we were ready to share with you not only the gospel of God, but also our own selves, because you had become very dear to us" (2:7–8).

One of their primary concerns has to do with the future. What about those who had died ("fallen asleep," 4:13)? The issue is not whether they will be raised at the last day. That assurance is clear. But will they miss the glorious appearing of the heavenly Lord Jesus? What will be the timetable of this "apocalypse" or revelation? Those people did not live to see the reign of the exalted Messiah disclosed to the whole world. Even if they are raised with all of humanity for the last judgment, they might never participate in the job of seeing Jesus' dominion revealed to a startled world. That was a sight they had dearly longed to see.

This was not merely an "apocalyptic speculation," in which people constructed charts and schemes of the future. This was a cry of those who have held firm in their faith in Christ's gracious reign in a world where it was not evident. Paul addressed their concern on the highest authority, "the word of the Lord":

For this we declare to you by the word of the Lord, that we who are alive, who are left until the coming of the Lord, shall not precede those who have fallen asleep. For the Lord himself will descend from heaven with a cry of command, with the archangel's call, and with the sound of the trumpet of God. And the dead in Christ will rise first; then we who are alive, who are left, shall be caught up together with them in the clouds to meet the Lord in the air; and so we shall always be with the Lord. Therefore comfort one another with these words. (4:15–18)

The Greek words for these events have now become loan words in English. The word "revelation" is a direct translation of the Greek word "apocalypsis," and the word "appearance" translates the Greek word "parousia." Paul never insists that this "apocalypse" or "parousia" would occur in his lifetime. The verses that follow in Chapter 5 refrain from any "word of the Lord" about "the times and the seasons" (5:1), and in other contexts Paul faced the probability of his death (e.g., Phil 1:19–26). Nevertheless, in this letter Paul apparently included himself among those who expected to be "alive" or "left" on this great day of the Lord's appearing.

The Christians who have died ("the dead in Christ," 4:16) will be the first to rise, and then the living Christians will be swept into the clouds for the reunion with the descending Lord. But the scene does not mean that the Lord and the faithful will spend eternity "in the air." The future reign of Jesus is not merely heavenly or otherworldly. Not at all. This "apocalypse" or "revelation" will be the disclosure of Jesus' reign on earth. And all the faithful will appear with him as the entourage of the vindicated Lord of heaven and earth.

In Chapter 1, we discussed the variety of expectations that existed in Israel about how God would fulfill the promised restoration. Chapter 2 demonstrated Jesus' distinctive concept of the kingdom of mercy, emphasizing the crisis that Jesus' program provoked leading to his death. Now Paul's proclamation of "the word of the Lord" articulated early Christian convictions of how Jesus is still the key to the future God has in store for Israel and the world.

Paul did not repeat stories of Jesus' life and ministry in his letters, but he consistently stressed the vindication of Jesus as God's means of saving sinful humanity. In Romans 3, Paul elaborated his conviction of how God's will and reign work. Jesus is again the central revelation of God's rule and righteousness.

God is still faithful and true (3:3–4), but God's righteous reign has been exercised in a most surprising way. Israel's wickedness has tested the justice of God (3:5), and God's Law has proved that all peoples, Jews and Greeks, are under the power of sin (3:9). Such "power" is a "dominion" or "rule" opposed to God, and thus God's Law has become a means for revealing human complicity with the powers alien to God. The Law of Moses or Torah can no longer be the beacon of hope for Israel or light of salvation to the Gentiles. It only illumines the depth of human sin; "through the law comes knowledge of sin" (3:20).

Paul was persuaded that God had every good reason to condemn all humanity, but that was not God's final purpose in Jesus. Destruction was not the future God had in mind, even if it could be justified. Once God's justice had been tested and had proved human fidelity to the alien powers of sin and death, God altered the exercise of this righteousness without compromise:

But now the righteousness of God has been manifested apart from law, although the law and the prophets bear witness to it, the righteousness of God through faith in Jesus Christ for all who believe . . . they are justified by his grace as a gift, through the redemption which is in Christ Jesus . . . it was to prove at the present time that he himself is righteous and that he justifies him who has faith in Jesus. (Rom 3:21–6)

This passage had long been regarded as the heart of Paul's proclamation of the gospel. It is "juridical" or "legal" language, filled with images of justice, judgment, justification, and condemnation. It presents a scene of Israel and the nations of the earth before the judgment seat of God, both now and in the future. It dismisses all human "righteousness," whether of Jewish observance of the Law or Roman morality. The only basis for hope in the future lies in trusting God's mercy at work in Jesus.

Paul's own need to "justify" his gospel, even in public trials, probably added intensity to his message. Both the Roman authorities and various Jewish leaders would have regarded this proclamation of salvation by the grace of God through faith in the Messiah as a threatening message. These were not "merely religious" issues in a world where Caesar's lordship and the centrality of the law of Moses were closely guarded.

Most striking, however, was Paul's understanding of how God rules. Without referring to "the Kingdom of God" or Jesus' radical word of mercy, Paul portrayed God's "righteousness" as God's will and rule at work through faith rather than through the Torah. Paul's argument was crafted more in the terms of the synagogue language of the rabbis, but its point was to confirm Jesus, and especially Jesus' death, as the definitive revelation and means of God's righteous rule.

Thus it is through faith in the rule inaugurated by this Messiah Jesus that humanity's future is secured. This is the new standard of God's righteousness, and this is the key to security in the future God has in store: not by keeping the Torah, not by acknowledging Caesar's divine authority, but by trusting the dominion of the crucified Messiah.

Both the Torah and the reign of Caesar have a secondary role at present. The Torah reveals human bondage to the alien power of sin, and God has given the governing authorities their authority as a terror to bad conduct (Rom 13:3). But no system of "law and order" could hope to usher in the promised kingdom. That future lies in the hands of God to be revealed with the full appearance of the judgment and reign of the crucified and raised Lord Jesus.

"Let the reader understand!" (Mk 13:14)

The Gospel according to Mark was probably written about fifteen to twenty years after Paul's letters. Paul did not date his letters directly, and none of the gospel writers identified themselves or the time they were writing, at least not directly. But Mark's story of Jesus appears to have been written in the midst of the greatest calamity of first-century Judaism, the Roman siege and destruction of Jerusalem and the Temple.

The most decisive clue is an unusual aside from the author to the reader in Mark 13:14. In telling Jesus' prophetic words about the Temple and the city and the "desolating sacrilege," the author tips the reader to "understand" what is being said. This aside also provides a fascinating window on the author's work as historian, narrator, and evangelist.

Mark 13 presents Jesus making a series of prophetic statements "on the Mount of Olives opposite the temple" (13:3). Much of this same material is repeated in Matthew 24 and Luke 21, with important differences in detail. The prophetic oracles and predictions are filled with scriptural phrases, especially from the Book of Daniel. When scholars read other Jewish "apocalypses" or collections of such oracles, they recognize an elaborate tradition behind Mark 13. In effect, Jesus is portrayed here as an interpreter of a range of apocalyptic phrases and sayings.

It is not possible to prove exactly what Jesus said on which occasion since even the gospel accounts differ. Yet no one would argue that he said, "Let the reader understand." That is the author alerting the reader that these words have special significance. Thus while recounting the memory of what Jesus said, the author was also concerned to communicate directly with the intended reader, probably a member of the author's own community. The author is also a storyteller and an evangelist.

Of course the future looked different by the year 70 because the world had changed from the time of Jesus or Paul. Like the earliest Christians and Paul, the evangelist was confident that Jesus was the fulfillment of God's promises to Israel. Faith in Jesus was the key to God's blessings of the future. But the opposition had apparently grown more adamant, and grave public catastrophes loomed large. Would not the full revelation of Jesus' reign as God's Messiah occur soon?

As noted earlier, Nero's reign was devastating to Israel, including the followers of Jesus. The unrest in Rome also provoked abuses and armed resistance in Judea. Finally, in 66/67, war broke out against Rome. A people with competing notions of God's promised future took up arms against the military might of the Roman order. Was this faithfulness? Relying on God against hopeless odds like the Maccabeans against the Greeks 230 years earlier? Was this a sinful refusal of the divinely authorized Roman order? Was this a means of divine judgment for a sinful people? Then what was the sin and what future hope remained?

Israel's past required a theological interpretation of this event. The Temple was especially crucial, as it had been in the Maccabean war, because here God's presence granted security. Josephus tells of a prophet named Jesus son of Ananias who cried woes against the Temple in besieged Jerusalem, and he repeats stories of portents of the heavenly armies abandoning the Temple (*War* 6.288–309).

The Jewish Sibylline Oracles, which also offered a theological interpretation of the calamity in the form of predictions, were actually written after the events:

An evil storm of war will also come upon Jerusalem from Italy, and it will sack the great Temple of God, whenever they put their trust in folly and cast off piety and commit repulsive murders in front of the Temple. (Sibylline Oracles 4.115)

The mention of "repulsive murders" may well have been an allusion to the assassination of the chief priests. At least Josephus regarded the death of Ananus as decisive:

I should not be wrong in saying that the capture of the city began with the death of Ananus; and that the overthrow of the walls and the downfall of the Jewish state dated from the day on which the Jews beheld their high priest, the captain of their salvation, butchered in the heart of Jerusalem. (*War* 4.318)

The followers of Jesus also linked the fate of the Temple to the agent of God's salvation, but for them it was the execution of the Messiah Jesus that was decisive, not the murder of the high priest. When the evangelist Mark tells the story of Jesus at the time of the destruction of Jerusalem, the links between Messiah and Temple are especially significant. The Messiah and not the Temple is the means of future security in God's plan from the time of the rending of the Temple veil when the Son of God died (Mk 15:38–9).

Mark depicts Jesus' apocalyptic predictions about the future as his speech "opposite the temple" (Mk 13:1–5). This discourse is a word of warning about false prophets at times of tribulation (13:5–8). It is a word of counsel about the necessity of suffering for those who preach the Christian gospel "to all nations" (9–13). It is also an alert that frightening and terrifying things will happen that could cause the faithful to lose heart altogether. The only comfort is, "I have told you all things beforehand" (13:14–23). Finally it is a prediction of apocalyptic calamity in the heavens and on earth, the final convulsing of the whole cosmos before the revelation of the dominion of the Son of man envisioned in Daniel (Mk 13:24–6).

Mark has depicted Jesus as an apocalyptic prophet, and it is clear that his depiction is deeply affected by his knowledge of the crises of his own era ("let the reader understand"). These dire events must be interpreted for the readers as within the divine plan of Jesus' reign. The fate of Jerusalem, grim and frightening as it is, does not prove God's failure to keep the promises. It vindicates God's judgment on the Temple and justifies God's Messiah, Jesus.

Each section concludes with a word of assurance, even when the assurance involves dire predictions: "This is but the beginning of the sufferings" (8); "he who endures to the end will be saved" (23); "then he will send out the angels, and gather his elect" (27). Mark's testimony restores the promise for the faithful. For those who persevere in their trust in Jesus' reign, the present tribulations are but signs of hope: "So also when you see these things taking place, you know that he is near, at the very gates. Truly, I say to you, this generation will not pass away before all these things take place" (13:28–9).

Every subsequent generation has wondered about how to understand these words. Clearly Jesus' own generation passed away, as did Mark's and thousands more. If it is correct that Mark was applying these words to his generation, was he wrong? Or was Jesus mistaken about his generation? (See also Mk 9:1: "Truly I say to you, there are some standing here who will not taste death before they see the kingdom of God come with power.")

Many answers have been given throughout the centuries, but none is more compelling than the last verses of Mark 13 itself (32–37). The evangelist has just depicted Jesus' words in the most immediate sense (28–31), heightening the reader's expectation that all of this applies directly now. Yet right then, he quotes the word of caution: "But of that day or that hour no one knows, not even the angels in heaven, nor the Son, but only the Father" (32).

This is an amazing verse, and its literal sense is often ignored by those who wish to use Jesus as a medium to predict the future. It also sounds a note that is heard elsewhere in the New Testament where the faithful are warned against assuming God's prerogatives (see Acts 1:6–8; Mt 24:36; 1 Thes 5:1–2). The caution is characteristically a word of Jesus himself in the midst of privileged revelation. Jesus' assurances about God's promises do not include a binding timetable for God; at least he does not know one, and neither do the angels.

Did the historical Jesus issue such a warning or is this a caution introduced by the evangelists? In either case, the Jesus of the Gospels and Acts of the Apostles cannot be used to unlock the secrets of a rigidly determined future. In his recitation of these most apocalyptic sayings, Jesus introduces an emphatic distinction between what he and the Father know. The specific urgency of his words, therefore, becomes an appeal for constant faithfulness and vigilance: "And what I say to you I say to all: Watch" (Mk 13:36).

Mark presents Jesus as an interpreter of Israel's prophetic and apocalyptic traditions. The future lies in God's hands, but God is contending with humans who are adamant in their opposition to God's will and reign. God's judgment and their persecution of those loyal to the Kingdom are fully predictable. Yet neither God nor humanity is locked in some fatalism or cosmic calendar. History, including the future, is a dynamic arena of the relationship between God's Reign and human will.

The warnings to the faithful are thus meaningful. These are not counsels of resignation, although massive forces and powers are contending (Mk 13:3–8). These are words of encouragement and appeals to endurance (13:9–13). They are also assurances of God's concern for the faithful in the midst of the struggle: "And if the Lord had not shortened the days, no human being would be saved; but for the sake of the elect, whom he chose, he shortened the days" (Mk 13:20). In God's good time, the future will be transformed into the arena of the revelation of the reign of Jesus the heavenly Son of man, Messiah, and Lord.

"This will be a time for you to bear testimony" (Lk 21:13)

The Gospels share the conviction that Jesus has been vindicated and exalted by God. The present and God's future reign are altogether tied to Jesus. But no single story is adequate to their understandings of this shared conviction. To the dismay and delight of Christian communities throughout the centuries, the New Testament preserves four stories of Jesus, each with its own sense of how that past related to later times and the days to come.

Mark's story of Jesus' words "opposite the temple" (Mark 13) is retold in Matthew 24 and Luke 21. These three versions are called the "synoptic apocalypse," and they invite very close study and comparison to see how each evangelist fits these compelling oracles into his larger presentation of Jesus. The Gospel according to John does not include this same material, but Jesus' extended "discourses" in John are filled with implications and insights about the future. Lifetimes of scholarly work have been invested in comparing and interpreting these varied depictions of Jesus and the past, present, and future.

For the present purpose, however, a few additional comments about Luke's story must suffice. Luke is especially interesting for three reasons: (1) Luke's account (like Matthew's) is closely tied to Mark's story; (2) Luke (in contrast to Mark or Matthew) identifies "the present time" (see Lk 9:56) as a significant and positive era of salvation in God's timetable in the midst of difficulty; (3) Luke's story of Jesus presses hard to link John the Baptist and Jesus into the prophetic history of Israel (Lk 1–2; 3–4:30; 7:1–35; 16:16; Acts 10:36–8) and continues on in the story of the mission within Israel and to the Gentiles in the Acts of the Apostles.

It is also necessary to admit that scholars remain deeply divided on how to understand Luke's story of Jesus and the future. The debate is lively because it focuses on Luke's understanding of history and of Israel's place in God's plans. Some argue that Luke is the gentile gospel, a story told at the expense of the Jews in order to justify gentile claims as heirs of God's promises. Luke and Acts taken together are then the story of the replacement of Israel in God's grace by gentile Christianity. This view has certainly been dominant in Christian history, where after the first century few believers were Jewish.

But Luke's story is being rediscovered as a Jewish–Christian narrative, a telling of "the things which have been fulfilled among us" (1:1). This is a testimony to how in Jesus God has kept and will keep the promises made to Israel.

It is important to note that the author never identifies himself and the traditions of his identity come from later centuries. Even the name "Luke" only appears in the traditional title of the book in the collection of gospels, "The Gospel according to . . ." Was this person a Jewish Christian or a gentile convert? Clearly he laid claim to the promises in Israel's Scriptures. And if he (probably such an author in that era was male) was a convert, did he come to the faith of Israel before or after he became a believer in Jesus?

Clearly Luke's story lays claim to God's promises to Israel, the same promises we have been following since our first chapter on pre-Christian history. Furthermore, this author regarded his "present time" as an era of divine restraint of judgment, a time when God "gave repentance" to Israel and even to the Gentiles (Acts 2:38–40; 3:19–21; 5:31; 11:18).

Most scholars also agree that Luke's "present time" was some moment within the last third of the first century, probably during the reign of Vespasian (69–79) or Titus (79–81) as emperor, or perhaps in the early years of Domitian (81–96). This was the "silver age" of Rome, in which relative tranquillity in the empire could not completely mask the years of violence and civil war that preceded. Greek and Roman authors pondered dark thoughts on "the delays of divine vengeance" for past sins, and the question of the meaning of history and the future required sober answers.

For Israel, these questions were excruciating. The Holy City and the Temple lay in ruins. The Romans had justified their cause and their gods in victory. They had displayed the sacred vessels of the Temple and the Torah scroll itself as spoils of war, and they led the Jewish general Simon in a harness in the triumphal procession of Vespasian and Titus to the temple of Jupiter Capitolinus. There they scourged and executed him in a chorus of applause and traditional Roman prayers (Josephus, *War* 7.123–62). The Roman triumph was as emphatically theological as it was military and political.

What did the future hold for Israel? The triumph over the Greeks centuries before had produced great hopes of restoration, followed by divisions in Israel over how God would enact this reign. Now surrounded by failed futures, blame flourished. The survivors could no longer rally to the Temple, the priesthood, or the Sadducean leadership in Jerusalem. The nationalistic warriors would rally one more effort in the time of Hadrian (ca. 132–5), but other Jews throughout the empire were eager to distance themselves from such adventures. Their survival was at stake.

The Romans had never shown much regard for Jewish theology or understanding of history. Their values of order and virtue and piety toward the state had little grasp of the "righteousness" of the Torah or little respect for the "Reign of God" envisioned by Israel. All of that seemed like "superstition" to them, or worse, like sedition, especially in the wake of the Jewish war. Even the Jewish historian Josephus repeatedly interpreted the Jewish defeat as due to disdain for Roman "humanity" and "virtue" (see especially his presentation of Titus' speech to besieged Jerusalem in *War* 6.323–55, 399–401).

Other Jewish interpreters were driven back into the Scriptures. The dire calamity of the destruction had occurred before, and the prophetic and deuteronomistic interpretations of that history were the first place to turn. Several of the Jewish books of this era even bore the name of an ancient worthy, as if they had seen all of this coming back in the era of the first destruction. Thus Ezra, Jeremiah, Enoch, and Baruch are brought forward as witnesses in various writings. The lament and hope of 2 Baruch expresses the anguish of the era well:

Do you think that there is no mourning among the angels before the Mighty One, that Zion is delivered up in this way? Behold, the nations rejoice in their hearts, and the multitudes are before their idols and say, "She who has trodden others down for such a long time has been trodden down; and she who has subjugated has been subjugated." Do you think that the Most High rejoices in these things or that his name has been glorified? But how will it be with his righteous judgment? . . . For there will come a time after these things, and your people will fall into such a distress so that they are all together in danger of perishing. They, however, will be saved, and their enemies will fall before them. And to them will fall much joy one day. And at that time, after a short time, Zion will be rebuilt again, and the offerings will be restored, and the priests will again return to their ministry. And the nations will again come to honor it. (2 Baruch 67:2–5; 68:1–6)

This is the piety of repentance that is confident that God's judgment is consistent with God's promises to Israel and the nations. It is the piety of Deuteronomy 32–4, as we saw in Chapter 1, and it is fundamental to the scriptural understanding of history and the future. Josephus, 2 Baruch, the New Testament authors, and the rabbis all shared this piety, as did most of Israel in the time of the Maccabees. But what was the sin that required repentance? Was it violation of Roman virtue? Was it neglect of the sacrifices or the execution of the high priest? Or was it the rejection and crucifixion of the Messiah Jesus? Which repentance and faith would yield future restoration?

Luke's Jesus spoke in strong terms of the coming judgment, and the Gentiles were the agents of divine wrath, just as in 2 Baruch: "For great distress shall be upon the earth and wrath upon this people; they will fall by the edge of the sword, and be led captive among all nations; and Jerusalem will be trodden down by the Gentiles, until the times of the Gentiles are fulfilled" (Lk 21:23b–24). There is no gloating at the apparent triumph of the Gentiles in this Lucan verse. On the contrary, it concludes with the same hope as 2 Baruch that the time of Israel's subjection to the Gentiles will have its limit.

Furthermore Jesus was not merely the predictor of that future. He was the occasion, the critical test. Only Luke is so explicit in identifying Jesus' "triumphal" entry into Jerusalem as the arrival of the "King who comes in the name of the Lord" (19:38). And only Luke stresses that the rejection of this acclamation was already the sign of Jerusalem's coming destruction "because you did not know the time of your visitation" (19:41–4).

The present time is not an era for the faithful to make charts or read God's mind about the future. This is the time to bear witness to the reign of the Lord Jesus that has already been inaugurated. That witness is to extend from Jerusalem to Judea and Samaria and to the end of the earth (Acts 1:6–8; see also Lk 24:47–9). The message to Israel in Acts was the restoration of the promise "to you and to your children and to all that are far off" (Acts 2:39), but this restoration and the ultimate "restoration of all" required repentance. And the content of this repentance is the recognition of Jesus as God's exalted Messiah and Lord (Acts 2:36; 3:17–21).

The thousands in Israel who come to repentance and faith in the early chapters of the Acts of the Apostles demonstrate the validity of Luke's hope, and the subsequent repentance unto faith of even the Gentiles (Acts 10–11) further verify Luke's conviction that God has already begun to lay the foundations of full restoration.

On the other hand, Luke is not a naive optimist about history or the future. The early growth of the Jewish Christian movement and the gentile conversions also produce opposition in a divided Israel, especially in the later chapters of Acts. The book ends with a very somber note of a third rejection of Paul's preaching by certain Jewish leaders so that the turning to the Gentiles has a strong measure of judgment. Israel and the final fulfillment of God's promises still hang in the balance at the end of the narrative. The future is as secure as God's faithfulness, but how it occurs will depend on the repentance and faith of humanity in the reign of the Lord Jesus Christ (Acts 28:23–31).

Chapter 4

Jesus and the End

The Revelation to the Heavenly Messiah Jesus

The revelation of Jesus Christ, which God gave him to show to his servants what must soon take place; and he made it known by sending his angel to his servant John, who bore witness to the word of God and to the testimony of Jesus Christ, even to all that he saw. (Rv 1:1–2)

Readers might expect this volume to deal with the Revelation to John in great detail. The shelves are full of studies of this last book in the Bible, and people often speak of "The Book of Revelations" as if they had just decoded a collection of apocalyptic secrets. Many Christians have made this strange book virtually the center of their Scriptures. Some people who practice arts of prediction and mysticism are fascinated with the Revelation to John even if they do not share its Christian faith.

The Revelation to John has long provoked controversy. For centuries, its inclusion in the New Testament was disputed, and objections were raised again in the time of the Reformation in Europe. Today, it is criticized for being too violent. Some suggest that it is a thinly rewritten Jewish apocalyptic tract. Those who use it as a codebook of the future are often intent on escaping or denying the present. But this is not what Jesus or the Christian faith taught. Have they correctly understood the book? If so, should it be excluded from the bible?

These are not idle questions. Those who eagerly defend the Revelation to John and those who criticize it agree on its power. But this power evokes a future full of both hope for the world and peril. Is this vision of Jesus and the future consistent with both what he taught and what the early Christians believed about him?

It is worth noting that mainline Christian groups have also turned to this book for a word of comfort in especially pressing times. The confessing church in Germany resisted Hitler's Reich with preaching on the Revelation, and contemporary Christians in South Africa and Eastern Europe are once again writing inspiring commentaries on it. Perhaps these interpretations offer a clue to the proper usage of this unusual book.

Our study must also recognize that this book is an unusual source for information about Jesus. The Revelation to John never claims to report what Jesus of Nazareth said and did during his earthly life. Even "the revelation" in the book was given to John through an angel (1:1; 22:6, 16). This is not a historical record of the teachings or prophecies of the historical Jesus. This is a divine disclosure of the heavenly reign of the Messiah Jesus. This revelation includes the assurance that his dominion will soon be manifest on earth.

Nevertheless, it would be impossible to understand the topic of Jesus and the future without study of the Revelation to John. This revelation is not only the last book in the Bible, it is also a distinctive testimony from first-century Christians concerning Jesus and the hopes of Israel. It is a stunning witness of faith in the future reign of Jesus in conflict with evil powers. No matter how cruel and demonic any dominion may be, the reign of the exalted Jesus, "the Lamb who was slain," is full of promise for the faithful.

Once again our study leads us to understand the present in the light of the future that Jesus' followers envisioned in his name. The issue with which we began was "Jesus and History," and we rejected attempts to speculate about the future or to deny the realities of the present. Those who merely want to decode the future will find no assistance in current historical studies of the New Testament. Similarly the Revelation gives courage to endure, not license to escape the present.

Our first chapter emphasized the "troubled times" in Israel in which Jesus was born. Israel's common hope in God's promises had been severely tried for several centuries, and various groups had come to envision differing fulfillments of that hope. The Greeks and Romans had found it convenient to play these expectations against each other, and even the Jewish Hasmoneans and Herodian kings failed to rally Israel behind a unified vision. The future had thus become a problem to present regimes, and those who envisioned alternatives to existing power structures had to be either disregarded or eliminated.

Our second chapter depicted Jesus as an interpreter of the prophetic heritage, stressing his radical understanding of God's mercy. The priorities of God's Reign were determined by the needs of the poor and outcast, the sinners and tax collectors. But if the Reign of God and the future belonged to them, what about those who were so intent on producing God's future through obedience to the Law? Those who believed that the future belonged to the ritually pure or to those who were willing to fight for it were also unhappy with Jesus. And the Romans could tolerate no dominion that did not sanction the future they intended to control. Jesus' proclamation of God's future and Kingdom marked him for death.

Chapter 3 highlighted early Christian confidence that God had vindicated Jesus and the future he declared. The first testimonies to Jesus' lordship, the writings of Paul, and the Gospels proclaimed this hope anew. The evangelists did not merely record what Jesus said. They told the story to testify that Jesus' life and death revealed the future God had in mind. Even as the Christians faced dire realities in the mid and late first century, their story of Jesus was full of hope. God's Reign had been inaugurated by Jesus, and he was the clue and means to the fulfillment of God's promises to Israel.

But in the Revelation to John, the crisis of the future appeared against a different backdrop. Christian faith in Jesus was not merely a challenge to other Jewish views of the future. This faith posed a challenge to the Roman order itself.

The author announced that Christians of Asia Minor were about to be denounced as enemies of the empire. Rome's claims to divine authority and virtue would be exposed in heaven and on earth as blasphemy. The reign of our Messiah would confront that of the great harlot, the scarlet beast in cosmic struggle. And what would become of the hope of Israel and the Messiah's reign?

The historical realities that the author confronted were harsh. This vision of the heavenly reign of Jesus was directly tied to the impending crisis for the faithful on earth, "what must soon take place" (1:1). The elaborate detail of suffering and persecution identified physical, spiritual, economic, and social threats. These were not fantasies. They were plausible responses of an ancient empire when its fundamental legitimacy was challenged. The Roman order could not tolerate charges that it was immoral, evil, or blasphemous. When its own stability was disturbed, it would respond with severity.

Scholars debate whether the Revelation to John refers to a specific persecution under a particular emperor. The most probable candidate would be Domitian, whose dominion began in 81 and culminated in a reign of terror in 93–6. Domitian's insecurity was written large in his adamant authoritarianism. He insisted that he be acknowledged throughout the empire as "Our Lord and God." The Revelation to John thus appears as an equally unbending Christian response to such policies. This book also fits an era when Romans began to distinguish the Christians from other Jewish traditions. But even Domitian did not undertake such a massive persecution as the Revelation to John envisions.

It is more likely that this last book of the New Testament was speaking about a general climate of hostility that was growing in the empire. And this book displayed Christian ada-mance in that situation. The problem was not merely a single emperor or persecution. The problem for the Christians had be-come Rome.

In the thirteenth chapter of Paul's letter to the Romans, the apostle had counseled obedience to the governing authorities. The thirteenth chapter of the Revelation to John recalled the horrendous vision of the beast in Daniel 7. Now the beast was Rome, "with ten horns and seven heads, with ten diadems upon its horns and a blasphemous name upon its heads."

In a fascinating return, the dire visions with which the Jews interpreted the Greek empire about 250 years earlier were re-vived. There the hope of Israel rested with God and the Son of man coming in judgment. Now the Son of man was identified as the exalted Messiah, Jesus (Rev 1:13) or at least as an agent of his judgment (14:14). Once again the people of God were con-fronted by a kingdom and a future that imperiled them and all they believed. This dominion also asserted divine authority, but the faithful utterly rejected this claim.

Interpreters have noted that the future that is envisioned is basically the same in Daniel and Revelation. The early Chris-tians have adapted pre-Christian Jewish apocalyptic. But this vision of the future was unusual in both traditions. It is helpful to recognize that the crisis was again severe. An empire that claimed divine authority had fallen into the hands of a despot who insisted on being worshiped. Like their Jewish ancestors, these early Christians turned to the Scriptures and traditions of Israel for their deepest assurances. But now, Jesus had already come. And the future that was revealed to "his servant John" was fundamentally grounded in the Christian faith.

How Long O Lord?

When he opened the fifth seal, I saw under the altar the souls of those who had been slain for the word of God and for the witness they had borne; they cried out with a loud voice, "O Sovereign Lord, holy and true, how long before thou wilt judge and avenge our blood on those who dwell upon the earth?" Then they were each given a white robe and told to rest a little longer, until the number of their fellow servants and their brethren should be complete, who were to be killed as they themselves had been. (Rev 6:9–11)

The death of the righteous had again caused the faithful to yearn for the revelation of God's Reign of justice and mercy. The future was not a subject for speculation or control. It was the arena where God's Reign would be manifest. Otherwise suffering would be unbearable. The meaning of the present was the urgent concern fueling the question of the future, "How long O Sovereign Lord before thou will judge and avenge our blood?"

It is necessary to observe again that the Revelation to John did not quote the Gospels or the sayings of the earthly Jesus. The central image of Jesus, however, was closely related to the Baptist's acclamation of Jesus in the Fourth Gospel: "Behold the lamb of God who takes away the sin of the world" (Jn 1:29). In the Revelation to John, it was Jesus "the Lamb who was slain" who is "worthy to receive power and wealth and wisdom and might and honor and glory and blessing" (5:12).

Here is the central Christian substance of this vision of the future Reign of God. The heavenly figure to whom all of the power and dominion of heaven have been entrusted is the one whose blood had been shed. The death of Jesus had established the standard of heavenly rule. But this reign stood in marked contrast to the dominions of the earth: "After this I looked, and lo, in heaven an open door. . . . At once I was in the Spirit, and lo, a throne stood in heaven, with one seated on the throne" (4:1–2). This rule had already created a kingdom of priests on earth: "for thou wast slain and by thy blood didst ransom men for God from every tribe and tongue and people and nation, and hast made them a kingdom and priests to our God, and they shall reign on earth" (7:9–10; see also 1:5–7).

But this new kingdom was far from evident. The saving reign of the Lamb and the kingdom of priests were under attack from "the beast." Instead of vindication, the faithful faced dishonor and death. The Christian vision of the future reign of Christ became the specific cause of persecution because it challenged the divine claims of the empire.

Once again it is clear that the topic of Jesus and the future has never been neutral. Ancient political systems had long perceived Israel's hope for God's Reign as a challenge. Jesus' distinctive emphasis on God's mercy also disrupted several Jewish conceptions of how God would restore and establish the Kingdom. Those who managed the present had a large stake in how the future was conceived. Early Christian proclamations of Jesus further stressed Jesus' execution as the ultimate disclosure of his saving rule. Now the dominion of "the Lamb who was slain" was set directly against the rule of the beast of the Roman order.

The boldness of this claim must be noted. The Romans surely regarded it as stupid or even immoral. The future belonged to the might and order of the empire. Abuses of imperial power were not appreciated by the Romans either, but certainly the gods had entrusted the rule of the world to the Roman system. This was a sacred responsibility, and the civil religion of Rome was essential to preserving law and order for future generations. Empires and governments may be more or less tolerant of religious dissent. But visions of a future demise of Roman dominion could never be allowed, certainly not in the name of one who had been crucified by a Roman procurator as a false "King of the Jews."

The author did not shrink from the confrontation. The first chapters of the Revelation include seven "letters" to churches in Asia Minor filled with warnings to hold fast against the sin of apostasy. Persecution and suffering lie ahead. God's promise of new life awaits those who endure in faithfulness.

All of this is a message from heaven. Future hope is about to be tested on earth, but it is assured by present reality in heaven. Jesus Christ who is "the first-born of the dead" has become the ruler in heaven and is thus also "the ruler of kings on earth" (1:5). But they do not yet know that. They will resist and kill the agents of Jesus' earthly reign until his heavenly dominion is made manifest and established on earth. The "time to repent" is running short for the adversaries and "the time is near" for the disclosure of Jesus' heavenly reign (1:3; 2:21).

If the Revelation seems eager for persecution, it is not because there is any pleasure in human suffering. The saints and martyrs cry for its end, and the Revelation is confident of the ultimate victory of the Messiah and his kingdom of justice and mercy. But this struggle is caught up in a larger drama of heaven and earth, of the present and the future. The triumph that began in the Resurrection and exaltation of the crucified Jesus is known only to the faithful. Until Christ's reign is manifest on earth in power, the struggle of the present is dignified by its place in the unfolding future.

The Kingdom of Our Lord and of His Christ

Then the seventh angel blew his trumpet, and there were loud voices in heaven, saying, "The kingdom of the world has become the kingdom of our Lord and of his Christ, and he shall reign for ever and ever." (Rev 11:15)

Israel had forged many visions of the power, mercy, and restoration of God's Kingdom in the complexity of a long history. Jesus pressed the tradition to focus on the heart of God's mercy. His words and deeds declared this acceptance and love to be the reign and future that God willed. The Gospels presented the earthly ministry of Jesus as the revelation of God's Reign and his Resurrection is its confirmation. Those who desired to understand the will and Kingdom of God must look to the life, death, and resurrection of Jesus. This was also the key to the past, present, and future of humanity and the earth.

The Revelation to John looked to heaven, but even in heaven the future was not simple. Time and history on earth were locked into events in heaven. The reign of the Lamb was not merely a fact. It involved a process and produced a sequence of events. Certain events had to occur in heaven before Jesus' gracious reign would be fully deployed in heaven and earth. Heaven had a future too.

That future was unfolding before the eyes of John and his readers in the Revelation. The cycle of images compounds the picture, with sevens following sevens reflecting the heavenly ordering within a world of chaos and peril. One by one the Lamb breaks the seven seals with each occurrence in heaven producing dramatic effects on earth (5:1–8:5). Each of the seven trumpets heralds new occasions in heaven and on earth, with an extended interlude of visions providing assurance for the human observers (8:6–9:21; 11:15–19). Even the delays give encouragement to those on earth of what lies ahead.

The seventh trumpet announces that the heavenly reign of the Messiah has now been established over the earth as well (11:15–18), and this event produced mighty changes in heaven (11:19). But the storm in heaven was not over, and the wrath on earth was still to come. It will be poured out on earth in seven bowls (15: 1–16:21), culminating in the judgment of the great harlot Rome who sits on seven hills, as on a beast with seven heads and ten horns (17:1–14).

This is a picture of how God rules in heaven and will reign on earth. But the opposition to God's Reign is gravely serious, even in heaven. The future of the earth is locked into a sequence of events in the heavenly realm. The announcement of the triumph of "the kingdom of our Lord and of his Christ" evokes worship from the heavenly elders. It also provokes dire portents and angelic wars in heaven that are soon driven to the plane of earth.

The Gospels presented Jesus as the revelation of God's future, but this disclosure was conveyed in their portrayal of his earthly life. The story of Jesus provided the key to understanding the present time within God's story. Events of the present were to be interpreted within this story. The future was the arena for demonstrating his predictions and dominion.

The Revelation to John treated the events in heaven as decisive, and the struggle and pathos of earth were but sequels in the divine drama. Horrendous human suffering was not a sign of Jesus' failed reign, but a test of the faithful in the midst of the battle against the forces of evil: "Rejoice then, O heaven and you that dwell on therein! But woe to you, O earth and sea, for the devil has come down to you in great wrath, because he knows that his time is short!" (12:12).

The immediate future was dire. It may be the time of "the judgment of the great harlot who is seated upon many waters with whom the kings of the earth have committed fornication" (17:1–2), but the great power, splendor and wealth of "harlot Rome" were still formidable. This "Babylon, great mother of harlots" appears "drunk with the blood of the saints and the blood of the martyrs of Jesus" (17:6). On the face of it, Jesus was not able to preserve his own from such evil splendor.

But the victory had already been declared in heaven, and soon it would be manifest on earth. The outcome of the battle was secure: "They will make war on the Lamb, and the Lamb will conquer them, for he is Lord of lords and King of kings, and those with him are called and chosen and faithful" (17:14). The entire vision, therefore, is confident of the future that Jesus finally will establish.

The Revelation to John is not fundamentally a book of predictions. Its prophetic vision is focused on the present time as the arena of conflict between the dominion of the Messiah Jesus and the Roman order. The future is surely at stake in this engagement because divine and demonic powers are contending. From beginning to end, the Revelation is a call to the Christians to endure in their faith in Jesus' heavenly reign and to repent for placing their security in any other power. Under the stress of Roman claims to divine authority, the Revelation insists that fidelity to God requires renunciation of the Roman order.

The Romans could never accept this view, although they understood the logic. A few years later, a Roman governor named Pliny wrote to the emperor Trajan with concerned reports about the rapid growth of the "contagious disease of this false religion." What was distressing about these Christians was their civil impiety. They refused to practice the public observance of the worship of the gods of the Romans.

Pliny was not intent on searching out the Christians, and the emperor agreed. But they were eager to offer Christians "an opportunity for repentance" and to give "pardon on the basis of their repentance." A statue of the emperor and incense were provided in Pliny's court. All that was required of those accused of being Christians was an offering and the cursing of Christ. Those who did not repent, however, would be put to death.

The matter sounds quite cool and procedural in the correspondence between Pliny and Trajan, yet it was deadly serious because the future of Rome depended on the maintenance of the civil order with its religious heritage. But such formal detachment is only possible for those in power. For the Christians, this was the crucible of life and death, of faith and the future. Thus the heat and passion of the Revelation to John.

The Romans and the Christians agree that repentance is the key to the future. For both, the present is also the fleeting moment for repentance. But the content of that repentance is profoundly different, as is the future it portends. Fidelity to the Roman emperor and faithfulness to the messiah Jesus now require repentance from the other, and two futures are envisioned. The one is the perpetuation of the Roman order. The other is the dawn of the reign of Christ that has already been established in the courts of heaven.

Heaven on Earth

Then I saw a new heaven and a new earth; for the first heaven and the first earth had passed away, and the sea was no more. And I saw the holy city, new Jerusalem coming down out of heaven from God. . . . And he who sat upon the throne said, "Behold I make all things new." (Rev 21:1–2, 5)

Our goal has been to understand Jesus today in the light of what we may know of him historically. This objective is especially significant with regard to Jesus and the future. Both the spiritual optimists and the historical pessimists often lay claim to Jesus.

Some take an almost perverse delight in their conviction that our planet is about to be destroyed in a thermonuclear holocaust. The fire and brimstone of the Revelation to John are eagerly expected as the Messiah's judgment. The righteous will finally be raptured away from a condemned earth.

Others discount all of this as apocalyptic imagery. The reign of Christ is a spiritual, heavenly dominion. The last judgment and the return of the Messiah have no connection with the future of this world. Whatever happens on the plane of human events, the reign of Christ has already begun in the hearts and minds of the faithful. The future Jesus portends is strictly that of individual forgiveness, the salvation of life in heaven after death.

Both of these views are foreign to Jesus, his times, and the testimonies to him in the New Testament. To understand Jesus historically requires an appreciation of the historical faith of Israel. The Jews surely spent centuries debating on how God would keep the promises in the Law and prophets. They could also become eloquent in their hope for the world to come, but their faith was always full of hope for this world that God created.

Our historical survey placed Jesus within this spectrum of views and common faith. Jesus' life and death occurred after a century of Roman rule. Still, the early Christian confessions, letters, the Gospels, and the Revelation to John proclaimed Jesus to be the fulfillment of Israel's hope in God, not its disillusionment. Jesus' teaching about the future and the faith in him as Messiah make no sense apart from his first-century Jewish origins.

We began with Jesus' crucifixion under Pontius Pilate, circled back in time to understand it, and moved forward in the first-century proclamation of his reign. But the "scandal of particularity" of Jesus' death and dominion remains. The future that Jesus inaugurated was the fulfillment of Israel's faith in God. That faith looked for God to save the earth.

Thus the Revelation to John ends with a vision of the ultimate restoration of God's Reign in Israel. The "new heaven" and "new earth" are images of renewal drawn from Isaiah 65:17 and 66:12. To say that "the first heaven and the first earth had passed away" is to suggest not destruction of the creation but its transformation by the glory of God's Reign.

The vision is so thoroughly Jewish that it shocks many readers. The fulfillment of God's promises is a new or renewed Jerusalem, a pure bride, in contrast to the harlot Rome. Instead of human emperors striving for divine honors, it is God who now dwells in the midst of humanity on earth.

Yet this vision is not merely adapted from pre-Christian Jewish apocalyptic. It is both thoroughly Jewish and thoroughly Christian. The Revelation to John understands the reign of the Messiah Jesus to be the fulfillment of God's promises to Israel. This is no mere prediction of what will happen in the future. This vision is a Christian restatement of Israel's faith.

Thus all of the symbolic measures of the Holy City are

taken, just as in early Jewish visions. But there is no temple in the city, for the presence of God and of the Lamb are the Temple. "The glory of God is its light, and its lamp is the Lamb. By its light shall the nations walk; and the kings of the earth shall bring their glory into it" (21:22–4).

Israel's glory had long been to be "the light to the nations," and this vocation had been one of the great images of restoration (Is 49:6; Lk 2:32; Acts 1:6–8). Now the restored city is also paradise restored with the river of life and the tree of life, hidden since Eden (Gn 2:10; 3:22). And the dominion of God and of the Lamb are exercised from the throne without opposition (22:1–5).

The world to come will come on earth, and God will establish the heavenly reign of the messiah among humans. In the Revelation to John, Jesus is the Lamb through whom God will exercise this dominion. The end of the story is not destruction, not even the end of the world. The end is the fulfillment of God's promises and the restoration of God's reign of justice and mercy forever.

The future is not simple or rosy in this vision. Great struggle lies ahead, even after a thousand years of the reign of the Messiah and his martyrs (see 20:1–10). The cosmic struggle of the reign of Satan and the dominion of the Messiah prevents easy optimism. Surely the experience of the awesome might of Rome also sobered Christian hopes.

Nevertheless, the Revelation to John was a remarkable testimony to faith in the future that God will bring. Israel's faith had taken many forms in the centuries of the Greek and Roman empires. Jews had often been pitted against each other in their understanding of how God would fulfill the promises, and those who were adamant in their faith at times found themselves in conflict with the official theologies of the empire.

Such conflict was clearly evident in the Revelation. Both the

Romans and the non-Christian Jews would find this faith in the Lamb who was slain unacceptable. Still, John persisted, confident of the ultimate triumph of this kingdom, but not optimistic about easy acceptance of this faith.

Those who find the battle imagery of the Revelation offensive would do well to remember the intensity and power of the Roman system. It is not surprising to discover those who have witnessed the shedding of innocent blood dreaming of bloody vindication. Neither Jesus nor the biblical authors thought that the Kingdom would come simply through moral improvement. The struggle is much more profound than mere historical progress.

The confidence in God's kingdom of peace, mercy, justice, and divine presence is far more remarkable. Here the Revelation shared the faith that Jesus, Paul, and the evangelists had in God's distinctive Reign. This is Israel's faith in God's promises, no matter how difficult life may be. Jesus had taught and enacted God's mercy as the definitive mark of God's Reign, and the early Christians had proclaimed this to be the future that God had inaugurated in Jesus.

In the Revelation, this faith confronted the oppressive realities of the Roman system and clung to the ancient prophetic images and hopes. This future would not come easily, and the blood of the martyrs would be shed. But the reign of Jesus had already been established by God in heaven, and this was the dominion of vindication and mercy of the Lamb who was slain. This reign was the future of the world and the hope of the faithful, living and dead. It was the hope of the restoration of the Kingdom and the fulfillment of God's promises.

The last words in the Revelation were thus adamant in their faith in God. The future that Jesus signified was assured by his own declaration to those confronted by imminent peril: "Surely I am coming soon." And between the final "amens," the seer placed all hope in the advent of Jesus' reign and pronounced the blessing of his lordship: "Amen. Come, Lord Jesus. The grace of the Lord Jesus be with all the saints. Amen."

The Revelation to John was an extreme version of Christian hope in Jesus and the future, but it was written to confront an extreme threat. It demonstrated once again that all of the early Christian convictions about the future were tied into the legacy of Israel's faith in God's promises.

For centuries various groups in Israel had held conflicting views of how God would restore the Kingdom. Their visions of the future reflected differing traditions and social settings. Jesus himself taught a radically gracious understanding of the Kingdom and future that God intended. His execution as "King of the Jews" was directly related to the future he inaugurated.

The apostolic witnesses and evangelists then declared that in Jesus' death and resurrection, God vindicated him as Messiah and Lord. Jesus' heavenly reign had begun, and it was the future that God had in store for the world. Toward the end of the first century, the Revelation to John confirmed this hope to the faithful who were imperiled in conflict with Rome. The Messiah Jesus and his reign were the hope and future for the world.

This historical study of Jesus and the future does not yield a list of predictions for the closing years of the twentieth century. Nor does it confirm or deny the forecasts of the futurists. Jesus himself appears to be more a man of his own time than most popular interpretations allow.

But understanding Jesus within his own era and among his own people has significant consequences. He belonged within a community where faith in God was fundamental to the future. He accepted the conviction of Israel that God's Reign would be restored and God's promises kept. That was the meaning of history and the hope of the future. He declared a kingdom of justice, fulfilled in God's mercy, and he inaugurated that future confident of God's vindication.

His program did not offer guarantees of personal comfort or untroubled futures, and those who proclaimed him as Messiah and Lord knew their conviction would provoke rejection. Then, as now, those who managed the symbols of power insisted that public order and national security be preserved. And their authority must be defended. How else could the future be assured?

But Jesus had announced and enacted an alternative future, a gentler reign where the cause of the marginalized, the sinners, and the outcasts came first. His vision of the future and his means for reaching it relied fully on the gracious will and Reign of God. His followers declared that his confidence had been vindicated in his resurrection, and they continued to proclaim this faith through a troubled century against severe opposition.

And this vision of the future has persisted since the New Testament era. It has been co-opted by empires, twisted into personal programs of success, and systematized into charts and predictions. But at its heart and in its historical origins, the future that Jesus announced is not subject to such control or manipulation. It comes by faith in the God of Israel who keeps promises. This future and its security are a gift.

Fear not, little flock, for it is your Father's good pleasure to give you the kingdom. (Lk 12:32)

A Note on Sources

Throughout this volume, numerous references are made to ancient authors and books that are not in the Bible. The citations correspond to standardized systems of chapters and verses used in all good English translations. Readers who are interested in investigating these sources should be aware of the following editions:

The Oxford Annotated Bible with the Apocrypha (RSV).

The Dead Sea Scrolls in English, trans. and ed. Geza Vermes (Harmondsworth: Penguin Books, 1972).

The Old Testament Pseudepigrapha, 2 vols, ed. James H. Charlesworth (Garden City, N.Y.: Doubleday, 1983, 1985).

For Greek and Latin authors and excellent translations of the Jewish authors Philo of Alexandria and Josephus, see *The Loeb Classical Library* (London: William Heinemann; Cambridge, Mass.: Harvard University Press).

Questions for Further Thought
and Discussion

Chapter 1

1. Why did Pilate execute Jesus under the charge, "The King of the Jews!"?
2. How did ancient Israel's exile in Babylon shape Jewish hopes for the future?
3. What kind of "consolation of Israel" did various Jewish groups expect?

Chapter 2

1. Why was Jesus' meal fellowship so threatening to some of Israel's leaders?
2. What was so controversial about Jesus' parables and "kingdom prayer"?
3. How was it possible for Jesus to preach both God's mercy and judgment?
4. What vision of the future is implied in Jesus' determination to complete his mission, even by dying?

Chapter 3

1. How was the memory of Jesus' execution as "King of the Jews" foundational for Christian hope for the future?
2. How did Paul understand Jesus as key to the future that God had in store for the world?

3. In what ways did Mark see Jerusalem's destruction as a sign of hope?
4. Where does the meaning of the present come from in Luke's understanding of Jesus and the future?

Chapter 4

1. In what circumstances throughout history have readers found the Revelation to John to offer them special encouragement?
2. Why did Christian faith in Jesus as Lord pose a particular threat to the Roman order in the era of Domitian?
3. How does the Revelation to John understand the relationship between events on earth and God's heavenly reign?
4. What are the specific hopes in the Revelation to John for the future of the earth in the end time of Jesus' reign?

Index